T0049807

PARENTS
WHO
BULLY

BOOKS BY ERIC MAISEL

Why Smart, Creative and Highly Sensitive People Hurt

Why Smart Teens Hurt

The Great Book of Journaling

Redesign Your Mind

Everyday You

Affirmations for Self-Love

PARENTS WHO BULLY

A Healing Guide for Adult Children of Immature, Narcissistic and Authoritarian Parents

ERIC MAISEL

CORAL GABLES, FL

Copyright © 2024 by Eric Maisel.
Published by Mango Publishing, a division of Mango Publishing Group, Inc.

Cover Illustration: Dedraw Studio, sudowoodo / stock.adobe.com
Layout & Design: Megan Werner

Mango is an active supporter of authors' rights to free speech and artistic expression in their books. The purpose of copyright is to encourage authors to produce exceptional works that enrich our culture and our open society.

Uploading or distributing photos, scans or any content from this book without prior permission is theft of the author's intellectual property. Please honor the author's work as you would your own. Thank you in advance for respecting our author's rights.

For permission requests, please contact the publisher at:
Mango Publishing Group
2850 S Douglas Road, 2nd Floor
Coral Gables, FL 33134 USA
info@mango.bz

For special orders, quantity sales, course adoptions and corporate sales, please email the publisher at sales@mango.bz. For trade and wholesale sales, please contact Ingram Publisher Services at customer.service@ingramcontent.com or +1.800.509.4887.

Parents Who Bully: A Healing Guide for Adult Children of Immature, Narcissistic and Authoritarian Parents

Library of Congress Cataloging-in-Publication number: 2023952613
ISBN: (p) 978-1-68481-490-9, (e) 978-1-68481-491-6
BISAC category code: PSY010000, PSYCHOLOGY / Psychotherapy / Counseling

Table of Contents

PART II | TOOLS AND TACTICS

Foreword

I tend to believe in the goodness of people, and parents in particular. Parenting is a difficult job, and children do not come with an owner's manual. So, we should not be surprised that some parents are ill-equipped for the job, weighed down by their own experience—or perhaps inexperience—and prone to taking their own early traumas or current stressors out on their children. Children naturally seek the approval of their parents, whether they carry the tools to offer it or not. Bullying of children is often the result, and the nature of the bullying is not always entirely apparent to the victim.

Clients I've worked with who have been bullied by one or both parents almost always express a sense of shame around it. Sometimes they feel as if they should have done something to either prevent or mitigate the bullying. They may rationalize the actions, suggesting that perhaps the bullying was justified because of their own misbehavior, or wasn't such a big deal because it did not represent the sum total of the relationship. Or they should not be affected by it to the degree they are. Or now that they are adults, they feel like they should graciously be able to simply let it go.

But a childhood of bullying is not eradicated so readily. In the wake of parental bullying, we will undoubtedly become symptomatic in some way or another. Depression, anxiety, eating issues, anger, and self-loathing may all be a part of the residual mix. Sufferers may find that their relationships with their own children or others are negatively affected. This is where Eric Maisel and his brilliant new book, Parents Who Bully, come in. The stories provided in this book allow the reader to recognize he or she is not alone. Many of us have suffered parental bullying, often in silence. Eric Maisel raises up and recognizes those silent voices, and allows their stories to be told, no doubt freeing others to tell their own.

What impact does bullying have on a child, and how does it manifest over a lifetime? Is it important to forgive a bullying parent? Should we distance ourselves from them as adults? And perhaps most importantly, how do we heal if we suffered at the hand of a bullying parent?

Compiling decades of research on authoritarian parents, Maisel describes three clusters of bullying behavior that will help victims identify and better comprehend the nature of their suffering. He provides thoughtful questions to consider while the reader journals his or her own progression with a bullying parent.

Over the past several years, we have been working hard in our profession to mitigate bullying in real time. People are aware of lying, cheating, double bind situations, gaslighting, and other forms of bullying and abuse that leave no physical scars but inflict deep emotional wounds. When a parent bullies a child, we are dealing with damage accrued years or even decades ago, when that child possessed little or no language with which to manage his or her feelings around the bullying, either in their lives or their own minds.

As clinicians, many of us feel quite helpless to aid the individual, child or adult, who suffered at the hand or at the word of a bullying parent. But in this book, you will find there are ways through the pain and trauma. They may involve rewriting your story, recognizing your power in the present, or forgiving the sins of the past. You may be inclined to work toward reconciliation, or find that a strong boundary between you and your bullying parent works better for you. Journaling may prove to be a useful tool, as well as telling your story to a therapist, reclaiming your story, and freeing yourself from your own sense of guilt and shame. Meditation and body work can help to heal your body and your mind. These methods are so important, to the individual, his or her family going forward, and our culture overall.

So, it's critical to understand the nature of your pain and how it manifests in your world today. The stories you'll read here will provide some examples that might help you stem the tide, and perhaps break cycles of abuse that have persisted up and down your family tree for generations. What a remarkable show of strength for someone who has felt hopeless and helpless for so long. What a gift to your own family, and to others.

—Dr. John Duffy

Author's Preface

I am writing this book for all the children and adult children out there who have suffered at the hands of a bullying parent or who are still suffering that way. The consequences of that suffering are profound and the subject itself is taboo; this is because the powerful write history and victims have their voice stolen by society's collusive agreement that those in charge—in this case, parents—write the rules. But we must not be silent.

The unwritten rule is that what happens behind closed doors is nobody's business. But it *is* our business. We must not allow romantic mythology about the natural goodness of parents to prevent us from pointing a finger at meanness when we see it. It is our obligation to describe in detail what parental meanness does to children, whether they are minors still trapped at home or adults of twenty or thirty (or seventy) who are still dealing with the lifelong consequences of that unfair treatment.

If you've experienced this bullying, you know that it has affected you. I hope that this book will help you to better understand those effects and will provide the tools and tactics you need for healing, growth, and recovery. I also want to paint a clear picture of the characteristics of bullying parents, characteristics that may have perplexed and mystified you. Whether you are thirty-five or sixty-five, it isn't too late to have the parental bully in your life finally come into focus. Let us look at him or her clearly in the light of day, and may shining that light reduce his or her power over you, if that power is still being exerted.

I did not experience parental bullying myself. I grew up with my mom, and we were a happy unit. But I saw how my friends were treated, and perhaps because my experience differed so radically from theirs, it forcibly struck me how unfairly they were being treated. It shocked me how minor infractions like spilling something or being a minute late to dinner could cause an explosive reaction, or how expressing a personal opinion might lead to parental rage and violence. Why punish holding an opinion? This was Brooklyn, after all, in the land of the free. Hadn't we just fought a war for freedom? Couldn't a child have an opinion?

The blight of authoritarian parenting has interested and concerned me for seventy years, since I was that child back in Brooklyn. It no doubt informed my decision to study psychology and become a licensed marriage and family therapist, and after that, a coach to creative and performing artists struggling to live the creative life. I hope that this slim book provides you with the tools and tactics you need to heal from authoritarian wounding, to deal with the bullying parent who may still be in your life, and to live with more ease and comfort. Those are my heartfelt hopes for you.

Part I

THE LOOK OF MEAN

Chapter 1

THE WORLD OF MEAN

Many parents are meaner than they ought to be. Whether it's because of stress, their formed personality, their philosophy of life, or other reasons, they oppress and bully their children. We have different names for these parents—we variously call them authoritarians, family dictators, bullies, narcissists, and so on—but the main things to know about them is that they are mean and that they number in the millions.

In this book, I want to introduce you to the horrible world of these family dictators. Let's start by getting grounded in a little history—the history of the idea of the "authoritarian personality." The "authoritarian personality" is a relatively recent concept. Starting in the 1950s, a body of research focused on trying to understand why so many ordinary folks were quick to act cruelly, easily meting out severe punishment to both loved ones and strangers; why were average people so often eager to follow dictators on the right or on the left, and more concerned about appearances than with doing the moral thing?

Following the cataclysmic events of the Second World War, researchers attempted to identify the qualities, characteristics, beliefs, and behaviors of authoritarian leaders, authoritarian followers, authoritarian parents, and others who, in one social psychology experiment after another, displayed an easily accessible inhumanity.

These researchers included Theodor Adorno and his colleagues at UC Berkeley, who in the 1950s coined the phrase "the authoritarian personality," as well as Stanley Milgram, famous for his learning experiments, and the contemporary Canadian psychologist Bob Altemeyer, whose decades of research provided an unparalleled look into what he dubbed "right-wing authoritarianism."

The seminal research on the authoritarian personality was conducted primarily by psychoanalytically inclined sociologists at the University of California at Berkeley. The name most associated with that research is Theodor Adorno. These thinkers believed that they had identified nine characteristics of the authoritarian personality (or, more precisely, nine characteristics of the authoritarian follower):

1. Conventionalism: rigid adherence to conventional middle-class values.

2. Authoritarian submission: uncritical acceptance of authority.

3. Authoritarian aggression: a tendency to condemn anyone who violated conventional norms.

4. Anti-intraception: a rejection of weakness or sentimentality.

5. Superstition and stereotypy: belief in mystical determinants of action, and a tendency to rigid, categorical thinking.

6. Power and toughness: preoccupation with dominance over others.

7. Destructiveness and cynicism: a generalized feeling of hostility and anger.

8. Projectivity: a tendency to project inner emotions and impulses outward.

9. Sex: exaggerated concern for proper sexual conduct.

The Canadian psychologist Bob Altemeyer, who spent his career researching various aspects of the authoritarian personality, identified three characteristics of typical North American authoritarian followers: authoritarian submission, authoritarian aggression, and conventionalism.

In the 1960s, developmental psychologist Diana Baumrind, reporting on her research with preschool-age children, described three parenting styles, one of which came to be known as the authoritarian parenting style. She described this style as characterized by strict rules, a refusal to explain the rules, the demand that these rules be followed unconditionally, and harsh punishment if they weren't followed.

The typical authoritarian—the typical family dictator—looks one way in private, but manifests another, sometimes completely different persona in a public setting. It is no wonder that victims of authoritarian wounding report that even up to the present day, they are *still* confused when it comes to making choices and doing intellectual work, as well as in their understanding of the exact nature of their authoritarian wounding.

Authoritarians often look good in the world, even very good. They can be charming in public and expert at reserving their authoritarian wounding for family members. This conscious, calculated duplicity is a feature of an authoritarian's cynical desire to get what he or she wants—primarily the ability to inflict punishment—without experiencing negative consequences.

Some authoritarians are authoritarian everywhere and are easy to spot because they are cruel and dictatorial wherever they go. But others look absolutely wonderful in public, and it's only behind closed doors that they wreak their havoc. We are going to look behind those closed doors at the lives and stories of the children they harm: the ones that they harm in childhood, and the ones that they continue to harm when those children become adults.

What appears to be at the heart of the authoritarian personality, whether that individual is a so-to-speak leader, follower, or (as often occurs) both, is a deep reservoir of hatred and a ferocious need to punish. Where this reservoir of hatred and need to punish come from is anyone's guess. No one can explain the why of it. Maybe authoritarians were born that way. Maybe evil exists. Maybe authoritarians were wounded themselves and are passing that blight along. What we can say for certain is that throughout human history and as far into the future as we can see, we will have to deal with family authoritarians and the harm they inflict.

You've no doubt heard a lot about bullying at school and about cyberbullying, but almost nothing about something at least as terrible, if not worse: the bullying that takes place in the home at the hands of cruel, narcissistic, authoritarian, immature, punishing parents. This bullying, which is rarely discussed, produces lifelong scars and ruins millions of children, preventing them from reaching their full potential and creating despair and high anxiety.

I am appalled but not surprised that so many parents are cruel to their children (and to their adult children). I am not surprised because it appears to be a constant of our species that a sizeable number of human beings, estimated by pundits to be in the 20–25 percent range, are authoritarian either by nature or training. Authoritarians are among us, numbering in the millions. So of course, they can also be found by the millions in families.

There they are, brimming over with hatred and a passion for punishment. In public, they may do a lot of smiling. In private, they are a terror. How could a child possibly make sense of this caustic reality, of how her mother or her father is so vicious and unloving? How can that child make sense of that actuality, even when he or she has grown up? Perhaps by hearing their stories, we can begin to comprehend the extent to which parental bullying harms our children. Maybe by shining a bright light on this abuse, we can help those who have been bullied as well as those who are still being bullied. Let us hope!

What will family dictators say about all this? They will say, "Stop your whining." "Stop bashing parents." "Stop acting all superior." "Stop exaggerating." "Stop lying." And of course they will say, "Go to hell." The bullies out there will rush to engage in more bullying. That is to be expected. That is what bullies do. Our job, however, is to persevere, to share the truth about family dictators, and to make the world a safer place for our children. Let's begin.

Chapter 2

ADVERSE CHILDHOOD EXPERIENCES

A newborn can't survive on her own. She comes not into the world at large but into a particular world, the world of her particular home. She arrives there with all sorts of attributes and potentialities, with her unique original personality. But instantly she is thrust into a situation with lifelong consequences. There she may find an overwhelmed mother, a disinterested father, a four-year-old sibling who is throwing tantrums, a harsh, noisy environment, and a culture that lays down all sorts of laws and rules. If she is lucky, she may fall into the lap of love. But she may not.

Where many children land is in a place ruled by authoritarians. I know this because I've studied authoritarian literature and worked as a therapist and coach with countless clients over four decades. But I know it more fundamentally for two reasons: because the adult children of authoritarian parents write to me all the time to share their stories, and because of what history has to tell us. It is simply absurd to suppose that we humans could have had loving parents and yet have collectively created the Holocaust, the Armenian Genocide, slavery, and the numberless other horrors we've witnessed, stretching from the dawn of human history to the present day.

The macro follows the micro. The same person who bullies his or her children will join movements that bully others. Since millions upon millions of human beings join and have joined such cruel, conscienceless, and punitive movements, we are right to suppose that much of what is going on behind the closed doors of family life is not very pretty. We may never acquire comprehensive statistics on that cruelty. We may never produce evidence-based studies that support the contention that millions of parents are mean to their children, and we may never be able to prove either in a court of law or even the court of public opinion that so many bullying parents are wreaking so much havoc. But we are right to conclude that the bullying and the havoc are certainly going on. History makes that clear.

We have adopted an interesting euphemism for the terrible things that happen in childhood. Those terrible things are called "adverse childhood experiences." Such a phrase is meant to hypnotize us into not quite noticing that one person is brutalizing another person. When a religious mother constantly and shrilly accuses her daughter of being in league with the devil and uses that as a reason to beat her daughter, as well as intrusively and constantly riding her daughter about every single thing she does, such bullying should not be granted an antiseptic label that goes in one ear and out the other. That should be called *brutality*, not merely labeled as an "adverse childhood experience."

Perpetrators, if and when challenged, will respond in one or both of the following two ways: "That isn't going on;" and "If it is, it's my right." We know exactly why they respond in such ways; we have heard these excuses and defenses since time immemorial. No remorse; no pity; no shame; no conscience; these responses reflect the everyday narcissism, sadism, and casual cruelty of petty tyrants. This is what is going on behind closed doors in millions of households.

Let us expose this through the stories of the victims, and let us join together to move mountains. These are societal issues, and, more fundamentally, they are species issues. For reasons that we could easily list, our species ranges along a continuum of kind to cruel, with the vast middle ground not looking all that pleasant. When the French philosopher Jean-Paul Sartre sardonically announced that "Hell is other people," this may or may not have been what he had in mind. But, as he had just experienced World War II and witnessed Stalin destroying socialism, this may be exactly what he had in mind: that we as a species are not to be trusted.

We should not trust that parents will love their children or treat them well. We can't provide the kind of oversight we might like to provide, but we can tell our stories. If you've picked up this book, that likely means that you've been brutalized by one or both of your authoritarian parents, that you know someone who's been brutalized in that way, that you're a helper charged with aiding victims of authoritarian wounding, or that the subject speaks to you, moves you, or interests you. You're likely open to acknowledging the hard truth that too many parents are mean. Let each of us, in our own way, do our part to combat the beast in our species—the meanness that in too many families manifests as authoritarian fathers and authoritarian mothers.

We'll begin by looking at the qualities and characteristics that we see in these bullying parents. Then we'll move on to hear the stories of victims, some of whom are still in the family home, some of whom have left their family homes years and even decades ago, and some of whom have buried the bullying parent, but not the harm.

Then we'll look at tactics for survival, creating as robust a tool kit of survival strategies as we're able to compile. We may never know why a given parent acts in the way that they do—we may never know if they are immature, ruined, evil, or what—but we can still paint a picture of how best to survive that bullying and heal from it. First, let's look this family dictator in the eye.

Chapter 3

WHAT FAMILY BULLIES LOOK LIKE

Statistics don't suffer; human beings do. Statistics go in one ear and out the other, yet one person's story moves us. Humanity is one story at a time. That's why I'll share a lot of stories in this book. I want you to see what real people have experienced. These are your neighbors, your friends, and maybe even your own family members. They aren't statistics.

If you ask them, "How are you doing?" they might respond, "Just fine." But that is a response that comes from their wearing their social mask and making polite conversation. The truth is darker: The truth is that they've been traumatized and may still be experiencing trauma. The truth is that they are burdened by the lifelong consequences of the tyranny they've experienced. What can they do to help themselves? We'll look at those strategies after we get grounded in an understanding of what family bullies look like.

For ease of thinking about all this, I'll be grouping the characteristics of family bullies into three "clusters": an aggression cluster, an exploitation cluster, and a narcissism cluster. Here are the characteristics and qualities you'll find in each cluster:

THE AGGRESSION CLUSTER

1. Hatred and anger
2. Cruelty and bullying
3. Punishment
4. Violence and assaultive behavior
5. Threats and scare tactics
6. Rigidity and obsession with control
7. Destructiveness
8. Impulsivity
9. Disagreeability
10. Domination
11. Sadism
12. Quixotic, unclear rules

THE EXPLOITATION CLUSTER

1. Intrusiveness
2. Manipulation
3. Shaming, ridicule, and contempt
4. Religiosity
5. Anti-intellectualism and anti-rationalism
6. Hypocrisy
7. Diminishment
8. Prejudice and bigotry
9. Preoccupation with sex and promiscuity
10. Cynicism
11. Love of chaos and disasters
12. Deception, lying, and truth as enemy

THE NARCISSISM CLUSTER

1. Grandiosity and egotism

2. Paranoia and enemies' lists

3. Superficial charm

4. Unacknowledged anxiety

5. Superstitions and mythic determination

6. Demands and coercion

7. Scapegoating

8. Lack of conscience and absence of guilt

9. Lack of compassion and empathy

10. Conventionalism and social status concerns

11. Submissiveness and cowardice

12. Loyalty demands

Not every family bully will display all of these qualities. One may harbor a lot of secret, unacknowledged anxiety, while another may be as cool as a cucumber. One may display a lot of religiosity, another none at all. But even though a given family bully may not display all of these qualities, it is good for us to become acquainted with them. They hang together logically, painting a picture of someone completely recognizable to us. You can't read over that list and not see the authoritarians among us.

I'll ground our discussion in real stories. For many years, I've been receiving extensive, full-throated replies to an "authoritarian wound questionnaire" that I've been circulating in cyberspace. I've heard from countless real people. In each of their stories, you'll see many of these dictator traits displayed. For instance, a story that highlights a bully's quixotic rules may also show off his cruelty, his sadism, his intrusiveness, and a dozen other traits that will become increasingly familiar to you.

In a moment, we'll look at these three clusters in more detail. But first I want to make a suggestion. You might want to keep a journal as you proceed through this book, a journal in which you think about your own experiences and what your own healing path might look like. Toward that end, I'll provide you with three journal prompts at the end of each chapter, beginning with this chapter. I think you'll find the process of journaling helpful and healing.

I've worked as a creativity coach for the past thirty-five years, coaching creative and performing artists on all of the issues and challenges that come with living the creative life. Let me briefly describe one client situation from my coaching practice where reflective writing helped my client grow in awareness and make important life changes. John, a British professor of history, had never finished writing any of the many books that he'd begun writing. I invited him to get some thoughts down on paper about why this might have been the case. He shared the following journal entries with me:

> I grew up with mean parents. After years of therapy, I think I've come to identify a kind of demon who comes into my consciousness and does not want me to be productive or successful. That demon was born in childhood. It somehow has to do with safety. It did not feel safe living with my parents, plus they *told us* that the world wasn't a safe place. They filled our lives with continual anxiety and catastrophizing.

> Here's how that all plays out now. My creativity starts to flow, and then anxiety floods in. I tear up the work, I tear myself down, and I abandon the project as no good. I'm also flooded with feelings of intense dread all the time, especially at night; and during the day, I'm always finding ways of

avoiding entering my writing space. And my writing space is easy enough to avoid, as I have classes to teach, committee meetings, a bit of a commute, and all the rest. It's supremely easy to avoid my study. And my study is so lovely. I wanted to write, 'lovely and inviting,' but it never does invite me.

In another session, he shared the following journal entry:

Those demons have made it harder for me to keep meaning afloat in my life, they've made it harder for me to keep despair at bay, they've made it harder for me to live my life purposes, and they've contributed to my anxiety and depression diagnoses. It's all of a piece. I've come a certain distance in all this and I can function, but I'm still searching for answers and I'm still wanting to finish some damned book.

I think that the bottom line for me is that the demon just won't budge because it is about core safety. Maybe I have to celebrate lesser forms of creativity where the emotional stakes and pressures are lower. An article, maybe, though articles aren't easy either! I haven't found ways to conquer the demons of darkness, but I do intend to continue to work on this block through some kind of inner demon work. I haven't quite given up. Not quite!

John and I worked together for the next three years, chatting via Zoom once a month. There were many downs, but also enough ups that John did manage to finish a draft of a book, deal with its several revisions, send it on its journey into the world of academic publishers, tolerate the criticisms and rejections his book initially received, enjoy the moment when it was accepted for publication, and so on. I kept reminding him, "This is the process;" and at some point, he began to laughingly beat me to the punch and become the first to announce, "I know, this is the process!" And throughout the process, he used reflective journaling and writing prompts to hold important conversations with himself and deal with the demons that were never going to fully go away.

Ready to start journaling? If so, here are three first prompts.

JOURNAL PROMPTS

1. Why are you reading this book?

2. With regard to one family bully in your life, describe one real experience with that bully...and what it felt like.

3. With regard to one family bully in your life, describe one consequence of that bullying.

Chapter 4

THE AGGRESSION CLUSTER

Family bullies are aggressive. Their aggressiveness is not restricted to destroyed furniture or beatings. It can look and sound very quiet. Still, whether loud or quiet, it comes from a hate-and-punish place and does real damage. Here are the twelve traits that make up the aggression cluster.

1. **Hatred and Anger**

   Authoritarians come from a place of hatred. As Max put it, "My father hated just about everything. His hatred was very different from anger or resentment or even rage. It wasn't an emotion, really, but a position, an attitude toward life. Anything could be hated, including things that he'd claimed to love and admire just a second before. You could fall from grace in a split second because he was so ready to hate—it was like hatred was always right there on the tip of his tongue."

2. **Cruelty and Bullying**

   Cruelty naturally flows from hatred. One of the long-lasting effects of this cruelty is deep confusion on the victim's part as he or she tries to make sense of what he or she did to deserve all that cruel treatment and what made him or her so unlovable. As Ramona put it, "I kept thinking, what am I doing wrong, what am I doing wrong. It made no sense, all that cruelty from both my mother and father over *nothing at all*."

3. **Punishment**

Authoritarians need to punish others. They are likely to advocate for capital punishment, for harsh punishment for all offenders, and to angle for punishment obliquely, for example, by adopting a "right to life" position so as to punish women for getting pregnant. They are always alert for an opportunity to punish someone, especially family members. As Mary explained, "My mother had an authoritarian personality, was angry all the time, and exploded just about every day. One time I fell off a swing and broke my ankle—and got beaten for crying. That's who she was."

4. **Violence and Assaultive Behavior**

Authoritarians are regularly assaultive and violent and often in a constant state of barely suppressed near-violence. Here's how Cynthia put it, "My violent grandmother successfully lobbied to get my mother committed in order to take over guardianship of me. My grandmother continually called me a whore, a slut, and a good-for-nothing, and told me that I would never amount to anything. I was removed from the home at age sixteen after my grandmother beat me with her cane and broke my collarbone for having a boyfriend."

5. **Threats and Scare Tactics**

Authoritarians want their victims to fear them. Robert explained, "I was married to an authoritarian woman. I always felt afraid of her. I quickly learned that she slept with a gun under her pillow, and on numerous occasions she threatened to kill me if I didn't do something she wanted me to do. We fought constantly, and she would always win because she was willing to go for the jugular and threaten to hurt me. I felt ashamed for being bullied by her and ashamed of myself for not leaving."

6. **Rigidity and Obsession with Control**

Authoritarians are aggressive in their need to exert control. As Barbara explained about a previous boyfriend, "When he spoke about his relationship expectations, they were presented as rules, givens, and truths that ought to be obvious to anyone. In order to monitor my compliance, he bugged our phone and put spyware on the household computer. When he 'caught' me asking a friend for advice about one of his behaviors, he responded by throwing my belongings into giant trash bags and insisting that I choose, right there on the spot, a destination for myself and 'all of my crap.' "

7. **Destructiveness**

One way to punish is to destroy. Authoritarians are destructive—toward individuals, toward whole groups, and toward objects, too. As Bill explained, "I was raised by an authoritarian father. He never hit us, but he destroyed objects like the television, the headboards of beds, and front doors.

His rages were terrifying, and my mother never stood up to him and didn't realize how sick he really was because he had a very fancy job high up in the New York City business world. If we questioned him, we were screamed at or ridiculed. He was interested in sleeping around and making sure we looked good—and when he didn't get his way, he destroyed things."

8. **Impulsivity**

Authoritarians, even when they aren't acting overtly aggressive, are on a short inner leash. Since they are so ready to hate and punish, they are also frequently highly impulsive: Authoritarians will "suddenly" and out of the blue aggress. Their impulsive aggression—that belt to the child, that bit of ridicule, that racial slur—only looks to be out of the blue; in fact, such behaviors are easy to understand, given all that simmering readiness.

9. **Disagreeability**

Agreeableness is a technical term in psychology, one of the Big Five personality traits first described by Allport, Odbert, and Cattell. In the literature, low agreeableness has been associated with selfishness, narcissism, antisocial tendencies, poor social adjustment, impatience, inflexibility, harshness, and an unforgiving nature. Authoritarians, whether overtly aggressive or publicly passive, love to not agree—they love to dispute, to quarrel, to deride, to ridicule, to just say no— because not agreeing creates grievances that then lead to opportunities for punishment.

10. **Domination**

An authoritarian will try to dominate wherever it feels safe to dominate or wherever his or her hatred is greatest. One kind of authoritarian will bully the weakest child in the family, because that child is the easiest target. Another authoritarian will butt heads with the strongest child because that gives him the greatest thrill. In both cases, he or she is coming from the same hate-and-punish place.

11. **Sadism**

If you are filled with hatred and a deep need to punish, and if you get pleasure from the punishment you inflict, that's sadism in a nutshell. As Wendy put it, "I always knew that my father's meanness had a sadistic streak running through it as wide as a river. He just enjoyed inflicting punishment much too much! At the same time, it was really creepy—everything he did had sexual undertones."

12. **Quixotic, Unclear Rules**

Authoritarians, who may or may not have any personal interest in abiding by rules, love rules for other people. The more quixotic and unclear the rules, the better, since quixotic, unclear rules are the least possible to follow. Such rules are inevitably broken, opening the door to punishment for the rule breaker. For an authoritarian, the rules are there *to be broken* so that punishment can follow. This dynamic helps to explain why an authoritarian is so often irritated to the point of violence when a rule is *followed*, since he was hoping for a violation and an opportunity for punishment.

Authoritarians are always just waiting to act aggressively. As Paul put it, "My dad could be sitting quietly reading the newspaper— and still you knew exactly who he was and exactly what he was capable of. It didn't matter if he happened to be patting the dog or whistling a tune—all that was needed for him to turn terrible was some stray thought passing through his head. He didn't need provocation, though he was always looking for provocation; he didn't need anything. He was a tyrant through and through—weak, sadistic, miserable—whether he was screaming or singing a show tune."

Next, we look at the exploitation cluster.

JOURNAL PROMPTS

1. Which of these aggressive characteristics does your parental bully most display?

2. Is one characteristic the most prominent?

3. Can you describe one incident that captures your parental bully's aggressiveness?

Chapter 5

THE EXPLOITATION CLUSTER

In this chapter, we look at the traits and qualities that make up the exploitation cluster. Authoritarians regularly exploit and make use of the people around them. Sara, for example, explained: "My parents acknowledge my existence and my accomplishments exactly insofar as it benefits them. They treat me as if everything I do in my life is for them to exploit for their own social or personal advancement. If what I'm doing or who I'm in a relationship with doesn't benefit them or conform to their idea of success, they actively work to destroy it and attack me emotionally, no matter how happy I am and even though I am an adult."

Here are the twelve traits and qualities that make up the exploitation cluster.

1. **Intrusiveness**

    When you combine an exploitive attitude, a need to control others, and a desire to shame and humiliate, you land on the following authoritarian trait: intrusiveness.

    Jill explained, "For me, the abuse inflicted on me by my father was not physical but verbal and also something else that's hard to define. He was always banging on the bathroom door or barging in if I was in there too long. He'd come in yelling, his face all purple. It was a crazy way of life with us."

2. **Manipulation**

Authoritarians are Machiavellian. Machiavellianism is one of the "dark triad" of personality traits that has been extensively researched by psychologists, who've developed measures to test for high Machiavellianism. What sorts of questions do "high Machs" agree with? "Never tell anyone the real reason you did something unless it is useful to do so." Ralph had this to add: "My brother had this cunning way about him from birth. Even as a two-year-old he could manipulate situations so that others got punished for no particular reason. He seemed to just simply enjoy seeing that happen. He wore a smile that you wanted to knock off his face. As he got older, he became more and more crooked in his dealings. What else would you expect?"

3. **Shaming, Ridicule, and Contempt**

To control is not enough; to win is not enough; to dominate is not enough: None of that is experienced as enough. The authoritarian wants you harmed, shamed, and diminished. As Samantha put it, "My father always looked at me as if I had no clothes on. I always felt naked around him. I don't know how he did it exactly; he didn't molest me or even touch me. But I always felt ashamed in his presence." Rob explained, "My father always shamed me in front of company. When we were at home, shaming me wasn't worth his time; he needed an audience. It was when we went to the house of one of his friends that he would delight in ridiculing me."

4. **Religiosity**

There are many reasons why authoritarians typically either are religious, claim to be religious, or get into bed with religion. Here are Larry's observations: "I got so sick and tired of my stepfather throwing what he called his 'bible rules' at me that I figured out a small test that anyone who's read the bible would be able to answer. I asked him a simple question. He clearly had no idea what the answer was; he exploded and gave me the beating of my life. I almost enjoyed it, because I knew that he knew that he'd been exposed as a liar and a hypocrite. After that, he still attacked us with his bible rules, but he was somehow much less convincing."

5. **Anti-Intellectualism and Anti-Rationalism**

The sorts of explanations that clear thinking, the scientific method, and the application of reason provide do not suit the authoritarian agenda. Therefore, it follows that authoritarians abhor education, especially science and critical thinking, and punish their victims for daring to think. Authoritarians who acquire political power immediately take direct aim at the academics, scientists, writers and other thinkers in their society, often terrorizing, killing, or forcing to flee even those professionals their society really needs, like its doctors.

6. **Hypocrisy**

Hypocrisy is a hallmark of authoritarians, who love rules for others but who typically despise them for themselves. As Ayanna explained, "My father was Islamic and a hypocrite. He expected us children and his wife to follow all the rules but broke many of them himself. He would pretend to follow some. Both he and my mother used physical violence against us kids. My father beat us regularly with a belt. He also got madder during a beating if we tried to protect ourselves with our hands or if we cried. My mother would always watch the beatings gleefully. But what stands out for me is the hypocrisy."

7. **Diminishment**

Authoritarians have a powerful need to discount your dreams, belittle your accomplishments, and make you feel small, inferior, and less than. As Deborah described it, "At some point, my authoritarian father sent me some of his old papers. One of them was a letter he had written to the Peace Corps saying, 'Deborah is not a leader.' Why did he say that when in my high school yearbook, I had twenty-six leadership activities under my name? And why did he need me to see what he'd written to the Peace Corps?"

8. **Prejudice and Bigotry**

If your motivation is hate and your agenda is to punish, you require objects for both. One fascinating result from research on the authoritarian personality is the willingness of authoritarians to hate and punish even members of *their own group*. Since an authoritarian lacks empathy, compassion, fellow-feeling, loyalty, and any other quality that might make him care about some group, his own group included, this isn't actually surprising. This hatred of and desire to punish whole groups—women, Jews, Blacks, Latinos, Asians, Romanis, homosexuals, the disabled, the elderly, and so on—plays itself out as prejudice and bigotry, two natural and inevitable consequences of the authoritarian agenda.

9. Preoccupation with Sex and Promiscuity

Authoritarians stand in some complicated love-hate relationship with sex. Roberta remembered: "The authoritarian personality in my mother did not emerge until I hit puberty. The second I began expressing an interest in boys, she became hypervigilant, watching my every word and my every move. She also became violently aggressive in ways that she had never been before, for example, smacking me with a rolled-up magazine that I'd been reading. It was like a monster had appeared on the scene."

10. Cynicism

Authoritarians hold to the view that it's a dog-eat-dog world. They cynically presume that everyone is essentially as ruthless, exploitative, and self-serving as they are. As Jack put it, "My boss had several pet expressions, all of them sexual and sadistic. One was, 'Do it to them first—and harder!' Another was, 'Come from behind—never let them see you coming!' His favorite was, 'If they're not screaming, you're not winning!' He made more money than anybody and frequently came on to his friends' girlfriends and wives—nothing gave him more pleasure. It completely matched his cynical picture of life that so many of them ended up betraying their man with him. That cemented his worldview!"

11. Love of Chaos and Disasters

Authoritarians love it when those around them are caught off balance and kept off balance. They therefore love disasters, chaos, and anything else that weakens, confuses, or disorients their potential victims. For example, Adam explained, "The first thing my father said when I lost my job was that he saw it coming, that I never should have chosen the career I chose, and that of course he wouldn't help me financially since I still hadn't learned how to stand on my own two feet. What stood out for me was how much joy he got out of saying all of that—my disaster seemed a gift to him. I haven't spoken to him since—and he hasn't reached out to me, even though my kids are his only grandchildren."

12. Deception, Lying, and Truth as Enemy

Authoritarians regularly use deception in order to exploit. Phillip explained, "My father, a pastor, baldly lied about everything from the number of people who attended his church services, a number he always inflated, to the crime rate in the 'bad part of town,' a number he likewise always inflated. It took me years to understand that every lie came from the same place: the place of making himself look better and others look worse. Then he could pat himself on the back and feel smug and superior."

Next, we will look at the narcissism cluster.

JOURNAL PROMPTS

1. Which of these exploitive characteristics does your parental bully most display?

2. Is one characteristic the most prominent?

3. Can you describe one incident that captures your parental bully's exploitive nature?

Chapter 6

THE NARCISSISM CLUSTER

Narcissism is a complicated concept since healthy narcissism is a developmental goal. Human beings ought to take themselves seriously, maintain a strong self-concept and a healthy ego, care about their self-interest and their goals and aspirations, and in these and other ways be "for themselves." On the other hand, there's unhealthy narcissism. That's taking self-love to the extremes of grandiosity, arrogance, and selfishness. That's where family bullies go.

Here are the twelve traits of the unhealthy narcissist.

1. **Grandiosity and Egotism**

   Whether or not authoritarians actually believe that they are special and superior, they behave as if they are. Zachary explained, "When my sister got married, my father gave the most amazing wedding speech—and he wasn't drunk and delivering something off-the-cuff, it was all prepared. First, he managed to ridicule the groom. Then he managed to ridicule my sister. Then, amazingly, he started promoting his legal services—his divorce services! People actually gasped and my uncle (on my mother's side) had to be restrained from going up and throwing a punch. Why ruin your daughter's wedding? There was just no scenario where what he did made any sense."

2. Paranoia and Enemies' Lists

Authoritarians, in part to explain their bottomless reservoir of hate to themselves, act as if they're continually threatened and endangered. They see enemies everywhere, including (and often especially) in former friends. As Emily put it, "My older brother kept an actual enemies' list in high school. It went with his tight, rigid personality; his anger; and the way he never fit in anywhere. He was so uncomfortable, awkward, and off-putting that naturally all the other kids wanted nothing to do with him—they gave him a wide berth. And so they got added to his enemies' list. He spent most of his time plotting his revenge on them."

3. Superficial Charm

Narcissists can appear charming. Ellen explained, "My brother was obsessed with his appearance—in all senses of the word. He was a real dandy, which was a pretty absurd look in our working-class neighborhood. He cared about how he smelled and was always worried about whether he looked or smelled sweaty. Yet behind all that sweet-smelling façade was someone who tyrannized my sister and me. In public, we were his darling sisters and he could charm people with his stories about how cute we were. In private, he hurt us badly."

4. **Unacknowledged Anxiety**

Often an authoritarian's rigidity and need to control others is caused by his or her unacknowledged anxiety. As Leslie put it, "To the world, my authoritarian brother looked like the least anxious person on the planet. But I knew better. To take one example, he couldn't travel on a special trip to Europe with his wrestling team because he was in a panic about flying. But he couldn't admit his fear and had to make up some preposterous story to get out of that trip. I don't think anyone ever knew that it was all about anxiety. By the way, he hasn't gotten to Europe yet."

5. **Superstitions and Mythic Determination**

Much of the hatred that authoritarians feel connects to their belief that this life has failed them and betrayed them. They deserved more; they expected more; they were entitled to more. The pain of this thwarted narcissistic entitlement is reduced by belief in a mythical future time when they will get their just rewards and their enemies will get their final punishment. As Henry explained, "My father loved that song 'Tomorrow Belongs to Me' from *Cabaret*, where that angelic Hitler youth sings to enthralled German beer drinkers. He also seemed magnetically pulled to every sort of occult thing, from astrology to the Tarot to you-name-it. He saw signs and portents everywhere, especially about calamities and disasters that were going to befall other people—which thrilled him."

6. **Demands and Coercion**

Authoritarians make demands as a matter of course and will do everything in their power, including using coercive means, to force you to meet those demands. Their efforts at coercion can include emotional blackmail, threats of violence, threats of abandonment, and threats of reprisal, especially from an angry god. As Anna remembered, "My mother, who considered me an evil and disobedient girl, continually tried to scare me with her religious notions. Even when it came to something like washing the floor, God got into it—he was going to punish me in the most horrible ways if I didn't get the floor washed perfectly. She was a real witch—or a jackal."

7. **Scapegoating**

Authoritarians scapegoat others. As Emily put it, "My sister loved to make fun of others, put the weak or the disabled down, make herself feel more important, and dominate every situation. Her behavior never stopped—throughout our lives she continued belittling others, pumping herself up and then, like the vulture she was, soaring down and making mincemeat out of her 'prey.' She ran for many political offices and won, too. She lived for power and control—all with a touch of sadism—and if anything went wrong, she had a whole list of folks to blame."

8. **Lack of Conscience and Absence of Guilt**

Many experiments in social psychology, experiments that have been replicated across cultures, socioeconomic classes, and genders with the same results, demonstrate the extent to which a majority of people lack a conscience and feel little guilt. When Hannah Arendt (in her book *Eichmann in Jerusalem*) coined her now-famous phrase "the banality of evil" to describe the Nazi war criminal Adolph Eichmann, she likely meant to convey this aspect of the fascist personality: that the evil they perpetrate is internally undramatic and produces no roiling inner conflicts, since they have no conscience or guilty feelings with which to contend.

9. **Lack of Compassion and Empathy**

Family bullies display little compassion or empathy. As Mark put it, "When a coworker of mine explained to our (very authoritarian) boss that he needed to leave early on a Friday because his wife was having a medical procedure, my boss replied, 'You're not having the procedure, are you?' It was in a way—in a horrible way—fascinating how consistent he was in his lack of compassion toward everyone. You could absolutely count on him not caring."

10. **Conventionalism and Social Status**

One of the most robust findings across all of the authoritarian literature is the extent to which authoritarians are conventional in their thinking and intensely concerned with their social status and with looking good to others. Rebecca put it this way: "My father had a phobia of doing the wrong thing around our rabbi, who played the role of friendly grandfather but who scrutinized you all the time. My father, such a bully at home, would panic if the rabbi even just looked at him cross-eyed."

11. **Submissiveness and Cowardice**

In authoritarian literature, there is a sharp distinction made between authoritarian leaders and authoritarian followers. Both are authoritarians; but they have their significant differences. One major difference is that authoritarian followers, for all their hatred, belligerence, and aggressiveness, also tend to be highly submissive, easily cowed by authority, and cowardly. As Susan explained, "My mother was authoritarian but more of a follower than a leader, although she liked to present herself as strong and independent. When it came time to prove herself and her strength, she never followed through and always submitted to the opinions of others. She always caved in."

12. **Loyalty Demands**

Authoritarians, though disloyal themselves, demand loyalty from those around them. "Loyalty" in this context translates as "the only one who counts is me." Respondents repeatedly reported that the authoritarian in their life demanded their unqualified loyalty, even if that meant endangering themselves. Max recalled, "My older brother stole a car. When he got caught, he demanded that I tell the police that I stole it. He took me by the shoulder and said, 'That's what a younger brother does for an older brother.' He actually had the gall to say, 'You know, nothing matters more than loyalty.' I looked him in the eye and said, 'No freaking way.' We haven't spoken since."

Next, let's see how these authoritarian traits play themselves out in the lives of the victims of parental bullying. It's time to hear some lived experiences.

JOURNAL PROMPTS

1. Which of these narcissistic characteristics does your parental bully most display?

2. Is one characteristic the most prominent?

3. Can you describe one incident that captures your parental bully's narcissism?

Chapter 7

BORN IN ALABAMA

Next, I want to share with you the stories of actual people who have graciously allowed me to present their stories. Each story highlights in its own unique way a number of the characteristics of the authoritarian personality. My goal in sharing these stories is to provide you with a clear picture of what victims have had to endure. Let's begin with May's story.

I am a female who was born in Alabama in the late 1970s. My father was quite the authoritarian. I was a very small little girl, and even at my full adult height, I was only five feet tall. My father, on the other hand, was a big man, six feet tall and weighing well over two hundred pounds. He was a physically imposing figure, and I spent my entire childhood and early adulthood in fear of him.

I lived alone with my mom and dad, and there was just no escape. My mother was pretty horrible too, but not as bad as my dad. And at least they never ganged up on me. If one of them was angry at me, the other one usually had my back. But if my dad was the one who was mad, my mom just let him abuse me and then she'd come see me later to comfort me while I was sobbing. She never interrupted his beatings the way he interrupted hers.

I used to tell this story for a laugh around my family until I grew up and realized I was normalizing and downplaying my own physical abuse and how seriously messed up that was. Anyway, here's the story: Dad liked to pull out the belt and whip me while yelling at me and asking me if I'd "ever do it again." And of course, I would always be sobbing and yelling "No!" but he would just hit me again and again. "You gonna do it again?" "No!" *Whap!* Rinse. Repeat. Finally, there was one time when he asked if I would ever do it again and I said "Yes!"—and he just beat the absolute crap out of me, but at least he stopped asking me the question!

So that was my life: growing up thinking it was normal for a parent to fly off the handle and beat me for the slightest infractions. I spent my young life walking on eggshells and not being able to understand why I could never do anything right, despite being a straight A student who didn't smoke, do drugs, drink alcohol, or have sex. There were no vices to remove from my life, but somehow, I was always a disgusting sinner or Jezebel or whatever.

My father was really into televangelists; he was part of the 700 Club and actually gave money to Pat Robertson and Jack Van Impe. He was intrusive and controlling. He listened in on my phone calls and read my diary and then punished me for things he read in there. He would eavesdrop on my conversations by lurking outside my bedroom door. He would force me to watch religious movies and pray with him. He seemed to enjoy punishing me. He would say things like, "This hurts me more than it hurts you," but he was lying. He looked for reasons to hurt me.

When I was fourteen or fifteen, my mom had cooked a pot roast one night, and I cleaned up the kitchen after dinner. There was a lot left and no storage containers big enough to hold all of it, and I knew my parents would freak out if I wasted any, so I just made some room in the fridge and put the lid back on the pot roast and left it in the original container. The next day, my dad "discovered" how "lazy" I had been when I was cleaning the kitchen and claimed that I was trying to poison them by storing the food in a metal dish. He said I had ruined the expensive meal and I was worthless and lazy.

He was screaming at me and forcing me to clean out that pot by hand. While I was at the kitchen sink cleaning out the pot, he was so enraged that he came up behind me and grabbed me by the hair—he picked me up bodily and threw me into the counter. My ribs were bruised for a while after that. My mother watched the whole thing. She was standing right there. She helped me up after dad threw me at the counter. I don't think my dad ever beat her, but she still never really intervened.

I developed a passive-aggressive personality as a result of the abuse. Any time I spoke up or tried to actively resist the abuse, it was quashed in the cruelest ways. So, I was quiet, distrustful, avoidant, and had a very impressive resting bitch face that I've never been able to get rid of since. I put up emotional walls and started becoming athletic so I could protect myself better. I immersed myself in books and video games and music. I was in choir and theater in high school.

I also threw myself into homework because I knew that my grades would be my best chance of escape. I was always in gifted and AP courses. I was inducted into several honor societies and things of that nature. It worked. I was accepted for admission to a prestigious university. I won a scholarship, and I went away to college and finally started living my life.

I remember one time when I was nineteen and back home visiting my parents during a school break, my dad attempted to physically abuse me again by throwing something at me, and I snapped. I just saw red and picked it up and ran straight at him and threw it back at his face and screamed at him to never ever throw anything at me again. I'll never forget his face when I fought back for the first and only time in my life. He looked scared of me. Good. I wish I'd been brave enough to do it years earlier. I packed up all my shit and threw it in the car and drove back to college within the hour. He never laid a finger on me again.

At some point, I was nearing graduation and job prospects were minimal. I was faced with the probability of having to move back in with my parents after college. After having a taste of freedom and safety, I was never going back to that life. I joined the military after college because having the means to stay away from my parents was absolutely worth the possibility of being killed. I figured I would either be living in another state or country, or I'd be dead. Regardless, I would never have to deal with them again. It was one of the easiest choices I ever made.

My childhood made me a very motivated and driven person. I knew I had to be successful so I could be independent and safe. I couldn't fail—it just wasn't an option. I became a perfectionist and control freak for much of my adult life. Now, in my middle age, I'm trying to unlearn all those unhealthy coping mechanisms, but it's slow going. I'm still struggling with automatic reactions that I developed while I was being abused, like when I drop something in front of my partner and immediately launch into apology mode, getting so flustered at doing something "wrong." He takes the time to calm me down and remind me that I'm not getting a beating—that accidents are okay and that I'm safe and loved. He is the best thing that has ever happened to me.

My father has been dead for more than a decade now, and the world is much better for it. There's this immense sense of relief that I will never have to see him again or hear his awful words or feel physical abuse from him ever again. It's incredibly freeing. Sadly, his death did not automatically undo decades of abuse, and I feel that I have been permanently damaged by exposure to him in my formative years.

But I am happy to report that abuse doesn't have to be generational. My daughter and I have a wonderful relationship. She has never had a reason to be afraid of me. She was never beaten or disrespected growing up. She became a lovely, confident person and never needed to be "disciplined" with corporal punishment to earn her compliance. She just didn't want to disappoint me because she wanted me to be proud of her. I am so glad that I was able to be the parent that I always wanted to have.

JOURNAL PROMPTS

1. Did your parents take turns bullying you?

2. How did you "escape" from your bullying parent(s)?

3. Was the parental bully physically imposing?

Chapter 8

DAUGHTER OF A BEAT

Neal Cassady was a major figure of the Beat Generation and the model for Dean Moriarty in Jack Kerouac's On the Road. *Here is Neal Cassady's daughter Cathy's story.*

We were having fun. I was visiting my mother who had "run away from home" when she was sixty and was living in the UK. She and I had taken an excursion away from her current home in London to see her old haunts in Rye and Winchelsea on the English Channel coast. After spending a splendid day seeing the sites, we headed to the train station to return to London. It was ten o'clock when we arrived at the station and were told we'd missed the last train. We had to wait until morning to catch the next one.

We went hunting for a place to stay, giggling and shushing each other like schoolgirls out past curfew. I felt the closest I'd ever felt to my mother. It was a wonderful feeling. We found a lovely room and giggled some more at the fact that we had no toothbrushes or pajamas. The mood was warm and comfortable the next morning. I was tying my shoes when my mother shouted, "You *hate* me!"

I had no idea where that came from. I was stunned and speechless.

"You have *always* hated me. Every decision you ever made was because you *hate* me!"

Mom was practically spitting in her rage.

"I don't hate you," I managed to whisper.

Her accusations continued.

She ranted. I protested.

According to Mom, I cried uncontrollably when I was an infant, not because I had colic as the doctors told her, but because I *hated* her. When I had my tonsils out at two years old, I gave her such a look of *hatred*, she never got over it. When I was three years old, Mom asked me to take care of my eighteen-month-old brother while she went out. She insisted I had purposely let him play with, and ruin, her pastels (she was an artist) because I *hated* her.

In shock and saddened by the sudden outburst, I followed her to the train station. Our ride back to London was uncomfortable and silent. I realized, as I considered her behavior that morning, that her accusations of me hating her reflected the fact that she hated *me*. At that instant, I knew why she had emotionally and psychologically abused me. I'd spent my entire life trying to please her, obviously to no avail. I had lived in fear of her behavior, including crying spells and violent "spankings." I have learned since that her erratic behavior is typical of alcoholics.

I remembered a phrase in one of my dad's letters to a friend referring to Mom: "She hates Cathy, endures Jamie, and loves the boy." (*Neal Cassady Collected Letters, 1944–1967*, ed. Dave Moore, Penguin Books, 2004, page 329)

Up until that morning in Rye, I'd tried to ignore all the signs. I believed mothers could not hate their own children. I thought I must be reading into her behavior. On that train ride, my mind went back to ways she had expressed her hostility toward me.

My mother's goal in life was to help humanity improve. She felt misunderstood when people did not appreciate her pointing out their flaws so they could change. Being the firstborn, I was the unlucky recipient of her philosophy in spades. My mother was critical of every facet of my life. I was never good enough, did not live up to my potential, and was lazy. She often complained I was "self-absorbed." She created horoscopes for friends, and the configuration of mine, she said, proved my selfishness. (Those with depression *are* self-absorbed.)

When I was young, harsh spankings meted out with a large paddle were a regular occurrence, but Mom insisted until her dying day that she never spanked any of her children. When I became a mother, she refused to babysit my son and had nothing to do with him if she could help it. I remember the time I begged to visit her on Mother's Day. She relented but was not happy about it.

One of the most devastating examples of Mom's ill-treatment of me was when she refused to tell me the filming locations of the movie being made about our family. Mom had written her memoir, *Off the Road*, detailing her twenty years spent with my father, Neal Cassady, and his friends, Jack Kerouac and Allen Ginsberg. The movie, *Heart Beat*, was based on her memoir. It starred Nick Nolte as my father and Sissy Spacek as my mother. I begged and sobbed on the phone with Mom, but she did not relent. She and my sister remained in Hollywood during the filming, and both became good friends with Sissy and her husband, even enjoying meals at Sissy's home.

It wasn't until I was older that Mom became more vocal about her feelings for me. These words are embedded in my brain:

"Let's pretend to love each other."

"You made my life a living hell."

"Stop that crying! You're only feeling sorry for yourself."

"You came into this life too soon. You still resent me from a past life."

Even into adulthood, my feelings were discounted. I don't remember hugs, affection, or being told "I love you." As a result of her control, I had no thoughts, ideas, or opinions of my own. My mother told me how to act, think, and feel. As a child, I had only one friend. The decades of incessant fear, the stress of trying to be perfect, and the unsuccessful attempts to please my mother all took their toll. I am seventy-five years old and still feel intimidated by authority figures, even when they are younger than me. I am trying to overcome the "learned helplessness" caused by my upbringing.

It wasn't until therapy that I remembered the self-soothing actions I took as a child. I wet my bed and sucked my thumb until middle school. At night, I would bounce my head back and forth on my pillow at night...right, left, right, left...on and on.

Despite having physical and emotional difficulties which I now understand were related to my stressful childhood, I forgive my mother. I realize she was damaged herself and yearned for a loving relationship with me. Perhaps she and I can have that in our next life together.

JOURNAL PROMPTS

1. Is it possible for a parent to hate his or her own child?

2. Did your parental bully hate you, love you, both, or something else?

3. Was there a split second when you came to a realization of what was going on?

Chapter 9

THE PLEASURE
SHE DERIVED

Here is Linda's story, punctuated by a history of suicide attempts. Do bullying parents derive pleasure from their bullying? Very often, yes.

I have few memories before the age of six. I don't remember playing, celebrations, stories at bedtime, family meals, or the birth of my younger sister. I do remember my pets, our television, and my favorite shows, ones that catapulted me into a dream world where love was real and magical things happened to good people.

My parents fought constantly. An average blue-collar household, from the outside looking in, we were the "perfect" American family. We moved across town into a new home just in time for me to start kindergarten in 1974. Small, sickly, highly intelligent, and with bright red hair, I was teased incessantly by the other children. I learned very quickly that going to my mom for support was a lost cause.

"What are you going to do about it?" was her go-to reply. I had few allies and no coping skills. I was obsessed with the idea that I could run away. One morning at five o'clock, I slipped out the front door and made it down to an intersection. In the darkness, I stood and watched the traffic signals change colors. It dawned on me that my escape plan was incomplete. I had no idea where to go or who to ask for help. I burst into tears and fearfully headed back home. By age eight, I attempted suicide for the first time.

Shy, introverted, and in a world of my own, I learned that my teacher wrote on my report card that I rarely participated in class. The A-grade I received in conduct sent my mom into a hysterical rage. She branded me a "chickens***." Ranting in a heap on the floor, she pounded her fists and screamed at God that she did not deserve a worthless coward for a daughter.

No one in the family was allowed to speak to me for the next several weeks. My sister and I passed notes. My dad would not make eye contact with me. I ceased to exist as a member of the family until my mom suddenly decided, weeks later, that I had been sufficiently punished. This event would haunt me for the next forty or so years.

From that point forward, my homework assignments were scrutinized, revised, and rewritten into language that was not my own. From third grade through high school, everything I created was picked apart and ridiculed. I was determined to get it right and to make my parents proud. I knew Mom needed me to shine bright in this world so she could feel okay. I also knew that if I shone brighter than her, there would be a price to pay. I lived on a razor's edge wavering between brilliance and mediocrity.

I was programmed to believe that my voice did not matter and that nothing I created held any inherent value. There was some physical abuse: a beating here and there, being locked in a dark basement to reflect on my crimes, or being forced to stand on a chair facing a wall for hours without moving. I was told all of this was "for my own good" and that my punishments "hurt her more than they hurt me." Poisonous pedagogy was the norm in our home.

Even as young as age six, I suspected my mom derived great pleasure from these humiliation sessions. Somehow, I was supposed to magically recover from this mental torture where my love, honor, and respect were demanded because these people were, after all, my parents. There was never any sense of trust or safety at home, resulting in an imprint on my tender psyche that screamed, "The world is a very dangerous place." I do not remember being told I was loved except in fleeting moments where my behavior reflected positively upon my parents.

It was not the physical abuse that was the most damaging. It was the emotional and psychological bullying that left lifetime scars and altered the course of my entire life. Never feeling worthy enough to step into my own creative nature and live as the artist that I knew I was born to be, I lived in a constant state of crippling competition and jealousy, with so many days, weeks, years wasted clocking time at jobs I despised and dead-end relationships, not writing, painting, or creating anything in my life that felt meaningful.

I self-medicated with alcohol, spent years battling bulimia, and engaged in cutting and other extremely self-destructive behaviors. I wavered between feeling fatally flawed or excessively grandiose with a burning desire to seek payback for my suffering. With no ability to self-reflect, I could not see those unfinished childhood gestalts repeating in my adult life seeking closure. I was perpetuating my own suffering, stuck in infantile survival modes, and desperate for someone to love me the way I felt I deserved to be loved. I was slowly becoming the bully that I so despised.

Two decades of therapy provided minimal value. I grew disgusted with telling the same stories. Spiritual practices brought some relief, and yet I still felt dead inside. The sad truth: I was and am loved, by many, yet I was too terrified to allow love and trust in my life. This "chickens***" had no idea how to alchemize that early branding.

In 2018, I wrote a short story. That story, infused with a seeking for clarity and peace, helped me to understand that my mom's behavior was a projection of her own internal angst, trauma and abuse, unfulfilled dreams and desires, and self-loathing. When I began to realize that I had embodied the archetype of the Bully and saw I had become my own worst enemy, something shifted.

I remember not being able to look in a mirror because I saw her reflection staring back at me. When I spoke with anger, it was her voice that I heard. I directed my focus of attention from her behavior back onto me, and I began to feel compassion for the first time. And so began the journey of my own shadow work using creative expression as the tool for embodying empathy, self-awareness, and forgiveness. That journey continues.

JOURNAL PROMPTS

1. Do you suspect that your family bully derived pleasure from his or her bullying?

2. Do you now feel safe? Or do you continue to feel unsafe?

3. Have you "become your parent"?

Chapter 10

ANY SADISM WILL DO

The sadistic smile of pleasure that we associate with sadists may be the only genuine smile that an authoritarian gets to experience, as it is only when he is inflicting pain and brutally punishing someone that he is really happy. Because of an authoritarian's preoccupation with sex, this dynamic often plays itself out as sexual sadism. But any sadism will do. Sadism is how a family tyrant experiences pleasure and release. Here is Martha's story.

My mom was the authoritarian I had to deal with. While her authoritarian personality didn't emerge until I was in puberty, it had a pervasive effect on my life.

My older sister was openly defiant and became destructively rebellious over time. I remember my sister screaming when my mother held her hands over hot burners to teach her not to steal. I also remember that my sister would simply toss her sanitary napkins in the bathroom trash can; so to teach my sister a lesson, Mom made a soup out of some used bloody napkins she gathered and forced her to eat some of that soup.

I responded by being the most compliant, respectful girl. I was terrified of what I was witnessing. I buried myself in schoolwork and reading, and I would have secretive nighttime revelries polishing off a large chocolate bar listening to music in the dark. I became a chubby preteen, and my mother took this development and ran with it. She would apologize for her outbursts of anger by conspiring with me and consulting with me on which cake she should bake for the family (my favorites of course) and giving me extra servings of dinner because I was a "growing girl."

I look back now and feel like I was in the Hansel and Gretel story, getting fattened up for future slaughter. This future became one of humiliation, taunting, and seeking solace outside the home in blessed fortunate situations where I would encounter healthier supportive surrogate parenting.

The result is that I have become damaged goods. One snapshot of the damage is a memory of going to my grandmother's funeral, knowing that my mother would be there. I begged my then-husband to not move from his position in the church pew between me and my mother. I felt that if my mother turned around and looked at me, I would be psychically incinerated. I was terrified.

I had successfully separated myself from some of the vulnerability by sheer will, taking the action of walking out with the clothes on my back and carefully crafting a life. It was a fragile shell of normality at first. I was shocked that my then-husband just smirked and changed his position in the pew on purpose, knowing how scared I was. I was so furious it became the undoing of our marriage.

I am blessed to have had much love and support dealing with the aftermath of being a witness to horrors—the terrified one surviving horrendous times. My ex had told me that when he relayed what he knew of my whole story to some experts, those experts told him that unless I was able to confront my mother, I would never be whole. Thank God that I had support, including the support of a therapist.

Eventually I called my mother to reconnect. She was bitter and venomous, complaining that my sister had been such a bad seed.

Right then I made my first ultimatum ever to my mom, indicating that she could choose to take down my phone number or we could disconnect. She got a pencil and paper. There is a long story that could be told about the rocky road of reconciling with a difficult mother. Let it suffice to say that when driving to the family house even after the first time back, I had to pull over to the side of the street and retch because it was so overwhelming. I should mention that the first time I visited the house, my mother came to the front door holding the collar of their Doberman, who was snarling and snapping. My mother commanded "Sic her" and let go of the collar—seriously.

All of this has been addressed in therapy, and that has been helpful. I've received depression and anxiety diagnoses; I'm a pack rat; I'm an overeater. Yes, I'm sure there's a direct correlation between all these disorders and being wounded by my mother. I know that I also had my own personal PTSD when I first left home; that was wretched.

At first, I failed miserably at college despite the fact that I am a smart, capable woman. I would experience flashbacks that Mom was coming to get me with the police to bring me back home. I'm remembering now that the first time I ran away from home during the course of a miserable weekend, when I came back home, my younger sister physically blocked me from leaving the house again. She had no idea what had transpired in my life and just saw me as being hurtful to my parents. She had such a different picture of the family!

I still have issues with anger. I freeze. I have been terrified that being angry myself would unleash destructive forces. I am still learning about healthy expressions of anger. As to any advice I have to give, it would be the following: Don't blame yourself. Give yourself time and allow people to love you. You will make mistakes along the way—love yourself anyway. Seek help when you are open to it. Life can be enjoyable, and you don't have to be in misery. This takes time—in many ways a lifetime. May your healing be a gift that you share with others. I was devastated to be disowned from the family will, but perhaps I have the best inheritance ever in spite of everything: I am intact, and I am living my life.

JOURNAL PROMPTS

1. Would you say that your family bully was a sadist and derived pleasure from punishing you?

2. Did that sadism have a sexual component?

3. What, in your estimation, have been the consequences of that sadistic behavior?

Chapter 11

HOW CAN I SURVIVE?

Each bully is a person with his or her own personal history and particular psychological makeup. In that regard, we hold each bully personally responsible. At the same time, it is true that individuals are born into a particular society, culture, and zeitgeist that is bound to influence them. If you grow up in a strict orthodox religion or culturally restrictive environment and then have children, won't that learned strictness translate into a bullying style that you as a parent can't help but think is both "normal" and absolutely required? And what if you are the child of those strict parents? Here is Emily's story.

I am currently struggling with my family. I am a seventeen-year-old senior, hoping to end up in a college next year. My parents are very strict Korean immigrants, and they are definitely authoritarian. We've been in countless fights with each other, and up until only a year or so ago, my parents were quite abusive. They have a strong mindset that they are always right, and that even if they are wrong, we must not call them out since children must always listen to their parents.

They do not understand that we are living in America in the twenty-first century, not Korea fifty years ago. I've been having nightmares, I had suicidal thoughts until just recently, and I've had severe depression for years now. My family has been to an untold number of counselors, psychologists, and psychiatrists. Several of them believe I have ADHD and am bipolar, though my parents refuse to believe it.

I don't know what to do. I've survived seventeen years with them. There are only months left until I am free from them. However, I'm not sure I can survive. I'm at a point where I don't know if I can continue on. Physical separation is impossible, given my room is right next to my parents' room. And if I go anywhere in the house, they get suspicious of me and follow me.

They've installed cameras everywhere. Psychological separation is also impossible. I've read innumerable articles, hoping I could become independent and strong somehow. However, my self-esteem and confidence have declined greatly, and I constantly think of the consequences my parents will give me whenever I do something. I feel like I'm trapped in a cage, and as if even when I go to college, I won't be free of them.

I'm stressed out about how I'll pay my college tuition, since they've firmly told me they wouldn't pay. They've constantly told me they want me to leave the house, but I don't have anywhere to go. I've been trying to get a part-time job as an online English and math tutor for pre-K to middle school students and as a flute instructor, since I'm planning on majoring in flute performance. However, it's hard to find students. I don't have a car or even a license, so I can't go and try to find jobs at stores either.

How can I survive? My mind is filled with thoughts like these, and I can't seem to get through life nowadays.

David tells a similar story:

I live in Brooklyn in a large Orthodox Jewish family. I think that there is a lot of love in my family and that my parents really want the best for us. But I completely disagree with everything they stand for, which is an impossible situation. I can't stand how my father treats my mother, I can't stand the messages my sisters receive, I can't stand the idea of a god who cares about whether meat and cheese are served on the same plate, and I particularly can't stand how the Torah is weaponized to make us "the chosen people" and everyone else idiots and enemies.

I've tried to speak my mind, but it's impossible. I can't go to the high school I want to attend, where I might learn the math and physics that interest me, but must attend a low-level yeshiva that is a reservoir of ignorance. My classmates are naturally bright, but what's on their minds is ridiculous. They can debate the fine points of Torah, but it's as if they lived in a cave. If I try to say something in class—well, that's impossible, too. It's like to hate dogma is to be anti-Semitic! It's crazy.

I'm bullied every moment of the day and night not so much by anybody's actions—nobody is beating me or physically harming me— but by my very environment; by the orthodox of our sect everywhere around me on Ocean Parkway when I go to yeshiva, in the markets, and at the kosher restaurants; by the clothes I must put on; by the loyalty I must show to our rabbi; by the distance I must keep from those not a part of our community... It's a bullying environment, with no one raising a hand.

I am not supposed to go to college. I am supposed to go into my father's business. Isn't that its own sort of bullying? I want to use my brain and do things that interest me and have a life, and that will not happen if I run a small business on Avenue P. So, I am going to have to make a clean break with my family if I am to have a life—as if that break will be clean! It will be a disaster and may lead to complete estrangement. Are those the choices a person should have, to be bullied into an orthodox life or to be abandoned by his family?

JOURNAL PROMPTS

1. Are you in a bullying cultural, social, or religious environment?

2. What strategies, if any, do you employ to deal with that cultural bullying?

3. How does your bullying parent use group rules and group norms to bully you?

Chapter 12

I AM LOST AND DO NOT KNOW HOW TO PROCEED

If you are still right in the middle of dealing with a bullying parent, you will likely feel, as Rob does, that you are lost without a clue as to how to proceed. Here is how Rob put it.

I live with my mom, my dad, and my brother, who suffers from autism. My dad is definitely an authoritarian. It's always his way or the highway. If your opinion is different from his, you are just simply wrong. Disagree with him long enough and he'll snap at you. He's a very short-tempered man who is incredibly controlling and needs to keep constant tabs on everyone and make every decision in the house. He needs to know every single detail of everything that is going on and to get the final say in every decision.

He's like this with my mom, my brother, and me. He's always had a wicked temper, and it's very easy to set him off. When he snaps, he will demean you, belittle you, and bully you. He is capable of spewing hurtful venom and does so all the time. The abuse I get from him is verbal and emotional; only on a few occasions have we had physical altercations, physical fights that weren't really much of anything. The problem is that he's also been great to me. He's been a great father many times. He's done a lot for me. He can be a great dad, but he can also be a terrible one. He's Dr. Jekyll/Mr. Hyde.

He can be a decent father for the majority of the day, but follow that with getting into an argument with a member of our family, stringing together a slew of awful verbiage directed at them, then apologize and make empty promises to do better. This cycle seemingly never ends. All I know is that I do not want to be this kind of father or husband. Other than that, I am lost and do not know how to proceed.

A STORY FROM A CREATIVITY COACHING CLIENT: THE COURAGE TO COMMUNICATE

To preview what can help, let me share a story about a coaching client of mine, a Parisian painter called Anne.

At the time we began working together, Anne was hiding out in Provence, licking her wounds after an unsuccessful show of her paintings at a prestigious Parisian gallery. She was barely communicating with the world and painfully wondering if she should continue as an artist. The facts that she has had successful shows and sold paintings previously, and that she was still something of a darling of the art world seemed to amount to nothing in the aftermath of what she dubbed "that monumental disaster."

We chatted over Zoom. One of my goals was to help her change her perspective. Her career certainly had taken a hit, but for her to dwell on that "disaster" amounted to not only a serious mistake but a recipe for despair. Focusing on that single event was only one lens through which to look at her career. I quietly and carefully explained to her that she was fortunate to have had the successes she had had, that this one event might or might not signal anything in particular for the future, and that her best path was to get on with her life and with her art-making—the act of which had fortunately lost none of its luster for her.

I asked Anne to detach herself from the show results. I also asked her to request some postmortem feedback from the gallery owner. How brave that would be, to ask him why he thought the show had produced no sales! She wasn't sure if she was equal to that. I explained that she might become more capable of that bit of bravery and feel more equal to it by doing some reflective writing, maybe on her turbulent childhood or her bullying father, a famous painter who always belittled and minimized her efforts; or maybe, in a more topical way, by writing about her feelings about communicating with Claude, the Parisian gallery owner.

We chatted a week later. It turned out that she had journaled every day that week using the prompt: "Do I dare write to Claude?" She explained that she had learned a lot about herself in the process, especially about her habit of fleeing at the drop of a hat. In childhood, she hadn't been able to flee. She had been watched, controlled, commanded, and punished for taking even the smallest step out of bounds. Now, as an adult, because she could physically flee situations, that's what she did—and far too quickly, she now understood.

Indeed, she returned to Paris, bravely met with Claude, and had that painful conversation. It turned out that Claude had very little to offer by way of explanation. People "loved the paintings." People were "wild for the paintings." Many expressed what Claude felt was a completely genuine desire to make a purchase. Yes, nothing had sold. But as Anne explained to me with relief, Claude was not down on her, had no intention of reducing her presence in his gallery, and in fact had expressed his intention to redouble his efforts on behalf of her and her paintings.

Over the months, I learned that several paintings from the show had sold for fancy prices and that her new suite of paintings was progressing nicely. She still had to endure all of the challenges that creatives must regularly endure, but her "monumental disaster" seemed to be behind her. "And I now have a sturdy tool in my tool kit," she explained. "I now have conversations with myself in writing where the part of me that wants a good outcome can coax my wounded self in the right direction. I now have a friend who is nicer to me than I usually am. And that friend knows all about my tendency to flee! She knows all about it—and she knows how to talk me out of running away."

JOURNAL PROMPTS

1. You may currently be lost—but can you picture yourself a little less lost? What would that look like?

2. You may currently not know how to proceed—but can you picture yourself proceeding anyway?

3. What strengths do you need to manifest, and what changes do you need to make in order to proceed?

Chapter 13

MY ACCOMPLISHMENTS WILL NOT BRING ME HAPPINESS

Many children of authoritarian parents try very hard to do what their parents say, meet their parents' expectations, make their parents proud, and excel at everything they try. When this doesn't get them what they crave—love, a kind word, recognition—their inner world begins to change. Some continue to excel while resenting their parents; others decide to fail, both because they are getting too little out of excelling and because they want to teach their parents a lesson. Here is Martina's story.

I was often rewarded with toys if I received As, and my parents would brag about me to my relatives, which only added pressure on me to be perfect. If I made a mistake or received a lower-than-expected score (such as a B+), I would be punished, reprimanded, and/or made to feel guilty.

When I was in third grade (about eight years old), I distinctly remember a time when my father was on a business trip abroad and I received three Bs on my report card. My mother called my father about it, which stirred great feelings of anxiety in me. I remember feeling very scared and sick to my stomach. When we picked up my father from the airport (he had been gone for days), he wouldn't look at me, hug me, or pick me up. I felt completely invisible.

My parents were also very religious, especially my mother. My parents are both Filipino and devout Roman Catholics, while I was born and raised in California. There was a period of time when we went to confession every week. I always felt like there was something wrong with me when I felt like I had nothing to confess. I wondered if I was "too proud" to recognize what I had done wrong. Surely, I'd done something wrong that week!

In one instance, I cannot remember what I did, if I'd "talked back," as my mother would call it, or something else, but I made her angry enough to demand that I kneel before her and beg for forgiveness. She then hit me with her house slipper. I remember crying, feeling terrified, and wanting to disappear. I then was forced to go to confession. I was grounded and not allowed to watch any TV or go outside. Try as I might, I cannot remember what I did wrong.

And so, growing up, I lived in constant fear of being yelled at, grounded, or made to study more. I sometimes resorted to forging my parents' signatures if test results were not up to snuff. I even forged a signature on a test I got an A on because I forgot to tell my parents about the test itself.

My hair began to change in fifth grade. It became very wavy and thick, and almost impossible to take care of. I remember my mother would seat me on her vanity chair, pulling hard as she brushed, and comment on how "ugly" I kept my hair. Comments on my looks continue to this day. She tells me to wear slippers in her house because she thinks my feet are ugly. If I've gained weight, she'll comment on it; if I lose weight, she'll comment on that as well. If I wear makeup, she'll tell me, "You should always look this way, you look much nicer." They're small words in passing, but they cut and cut and cut.

Due to their religiosity, I was often told by my parents that whatever I achieved or was talented in was because I was "blessed" and that I should be "grateful to God." But if I fell short of their expectations, it was always because of some failing on my part. I had and continue to have issues with confidence and self-worth. Beyond this, I have come to dislike and distrust organized religion.

As a girl, I had to be modest in both personality as well as attire. I could not show "too much skin." My mother would frequently "cover me up" in public or force me to tuck my shirt in, and sometimes she would say out loud, "You stink." My father, on the other hand, was disappointed in me for playing with makeup and trying nail polish at thirteen. In college, when I decided to dye my hair another color, both my parents said I embarrassed them.

But grades and looks were not the only thing under the microscope. On more than one occasion, my mother commented that she "didn't like" my friend. One of those friends was my best friend, whom I left behind after we moved to another city. She would call me almost every day. This irritated my mother to the point that she shook the phone in her hand and yelled, "Why is she always calling you and calling you?" I began to cry and said, "We're best friends. I miss her." She responded by grabbing my shoulder, shaking me, and yelling at me to "Stop it! Shut up!"

In high school, my father disapproved of even the idea of a boyfriend. Grades came first and foremost. Yet it was in high school that my grades began to collapse. I was burned out. I didn't care anymore, and I found myself often wishing to die. At sixteen, my best friend in high school was asked to prom. I had a very deep crush on this girl and felt no ill will toward her or the boy who asked her out. But I still felt unable to go to prom or enjoy it without a date. I turned to my mother for support, and she said, "Well, that's why girls can't be friends forever. There's always jealousy." My mother didn't touch me or hug me or comfort me. I honestly don't feel like I can tell her anything. I've stopped telling her anything, and yet she wonders why I never call her except on her birthday and on Mother's Day.

Having so many things in my life chosen or decided for me tried my patience. I felt as though I was living in a box with only a single window from which I could watch my peers and on occasion receive praise and rewards if I performed as commanded. Because my parents helped me to afford it, I was able to study writing in college; and to this day, I feel guilty for resenting my parents for their treatment of me, despite their efforts and sacrifices to pay for my dreams. There's a persistent feeling that I will never be validated, that I will never have a victory to call my own. I keep yearning for the day that I will achieve something of great significance and be recognized for it, but I am aware of the fact that even if I accomplish such a thing, it will not bring me happiness.

JOURNAL PROMPTS

1. Did you excel because it was demanded of you that you excel?

2. Did you rebel and "act out" and refuse to excel?

3. Is there any possible accomplishment that will bring you happiness?

Chapter 14

THE SHAMING BEGAN

Bullying parents routinely shame their children, if not in public, then in private. Here is Sylvia's story.

One of my earliest memories as a child was when I was playing with another child in our living room. I can't remember who I was playing with or what we were doing, but my mother pulled me up by the arm and yelled at me, "Why did you do that?!" I told her I didn't know, because honestly, as a two-year-old or three-year-old child, I didn't know why I did anything. She kept asking me why I did whatever it was I did, and I kept saying I didn't know.

I can't remember if she hit me, but she did sit me down in our brown armchair in the corner of the room and continued to ask the same question, with me giving the same answer. She told me that if I said, "I don't know" one more time, something would happen, maybe a smack, I can't remember. So, when she asked me again, I stopped talking. She walked away from me, and I remember looking down into my lap feeling ashamed of myself for being "bad," upset that I didn't have another answer for her, and horrible for having upset her. It is one of the earliest memories I have of internalizing shame.

I have another memory of my brother and I sitting across from each other at the kitchen table, laughing and eating cereal as we always did every morning. We were probably around ten years old. My mother walked into the kitchen and spotted perhaps six tiny dots of orange juice splattered on her white wall, an easily washable blot on its perfection. She demanded to know who had done this. We froze and didn't speak.

I sat there frantically trying to recall if it had been me; I thought maybe it had been, but I just couldn't recall. She continued to demand over and over who had done it, and I became more and more anxious. Finally, my brother burst into tears and yelled in shame, "It was me!" My mother hit him repeatedly on his body and maybe even his head. I felt horrible for my brother, but I stared into my cereal as it happened.

My brother and I were latchkey kids, and we would come home from middle school and early high school and plant ourselves in front of the TV until my mother came home. I still remember how every time my mother walked through the back door and yelled, "Hello!" I would listen for the tone of her voice. Was it happy? Phew, I could relax. Was it annoyed? Had she had a bad day at work? My anxiety would go through the roof waiting for her to take out her short temper on us.

As a teenager, I remember one time she told me to sweep the floor of the kitchen. I grabbed the broom and began sweeping, doing so in the best way I could. She grabbed the broom out of my hand and said something like, "What are you doing? What, are you left-handed? You need to sweep like *this*!" and proceeded to make me sweep *her* way, which was right-handed.

I didn't really see the difference at all. The floor still got swept, except now I felt bad that I hadn't been doing it the "right" way. To her, everything had a right way and a wrong way, and everyone was either good or bad. And whatever she declared to be right or wrong, bad or good, was law in the house. Deviation from this meant shaming and sometimes hitting. To this day, I still sweep the floor using both left-handed and right-handed sweeping, switching back and forth as needed.

As I got into high school, I began challenging her more. I realized that her unfair treatment of us was mean, tyrannical, and extremely rigid. When I tried to challenge her irrational rules and her meanness, even if I did it calmly, she would guilt me by saying, "How dare you speak to me like that?!" If the discussion became heated, even if I hadn't used curse words or said anything really aggressive, she would slap me across the face just for disagreeing.

A few times she tricked me into opening up in a heart-to-heart conversation. Each time, she came into my room while I was crying, asking me what was wrong. She manipulated me, saying I could always talk to her, that she would help me. I remember one time I finally told her how much something she said hurt me. Her comforting demeanor immediately turned into defensiveness. She gaslighted me by telling me what I said had never happened and that I shouldn't feel the way I felt.

She would gaslight me about her hitting me and saying mean things to me, or about how events had unfolded, and still continues to do so to this day. And then she would tell me she loved me so much. I would feel so confused because I certainly didn't feel loved. And I would cry and cry, not understanding why I was such a bad daughter, why I was so crazy, why I felt so alone.

As an adult, I only visit her a few times a year on holidays and birthdays. For a long time, when I would visit her, everything would seem to go well for a few days; but inevitably, on about day three, her mood would turn sour. She would begin picking out things we weren't doing right, and small things would become huge to her. Screaming fights and hitting ensued. I learned that I couldn't stay with her for more than two days.

In essence, unquestioning obedience was the rule of law. Nothing could be discussed, or it was labeled "back talk." Mistakes were met with swift physical and emotional abuse. I was always anxious and hypervigilant, a habitual response that tortures me, and one I can't shake even now that I'm thirty-seven years old. I see my mother twice a year, and even those times are hard because any small sign of her disapproval, any small brow furrow, any tone in her voice makes my anxiety shoot through the roof. I struggle to trust people, I crumble in front of any authority figure, I constantly look out for something bad that might happen, and generally I just don't feel like I am a good person.

JOURNAL PROMPTS

1. Did your bullying parent shame you?

2. If you can remember, when did the shaming begin?

3. Do you still feel ashamed to this day?

Chapter 15

AN EMPTY SHELL

It is hard to capture the emptiness at the heart of an authoritarian's being. Bullies are often both physically intimidating and not really present, as if they were ghosts inhabiting suits of armor. Here is Nancy's take on this strange phenomenon.

My mother grew up in Nazi Germany and shared their authoritarian beliefs, as well as their sense of victimhood. My father was American but held similar beliefs, although of the two, he was more creative and occasionally more generous than my mother. I think he bought all the victim stories coming from my mother, but he was definitely conservative himself. My family is extreme right-wing Catholic. I see varying degrees of authoritarianism in my siblings today: a serious stockpiling of guns by one brother, while a second brother is head of the now dormant America First party. My sister is the least authoritarian of my four siblings. I have a third brother who is a born-again Christian.

I knew at a young age that there was something very wrong in my family. I had read about the typical authoritarian's desire to punish, and that was my experience with them, that they were always looking for reasons to punish me. It was an ongoing event, from physical abuse to verbal abuse, from the loss of lots of privileges to a general withholding of anything that mattered or would be a source of joy.

I tried to tell people about it, and I was ridiculed because both my parents were very good at marketing themselves to others.

Basically, my childhood was miserable. I was expected to anticipate and meet everyone's needs. I was not allowed any needs of my own. If I formed relationships outside the home, they were squashed. Throughout my childhood, I worked all the time and was pretty much a prisoner. I believe that one objective of authoritarians is to get you to shut down so that they can take you over. Thinking for myself and trying to understand my situation helped me a little, but only a very little.

My mother was authoritarian through and through, although she was also very good at playing the victim; my father, too. They were two mean victims! They seemed to creatively expand on their own victimization as an excuse to punish and to scapegoat. They were also very ambitious and wanted to get the world to live by their ideas. Part of their plan was to create a media empire for their right-wing ideas. They were not successful. My father was indicted for Medicare fraud and convicted, and he went to jail for it. So much for building their empire!

I think that because of my childhood experiences, I've lost a lot of my desire to have much of anything. Growing up, the cost of wanting anything far outweighed any benefits because of the punishments that came with those desires. I was told that I could choose either what I wanted or what they wanted—the choice was mine—but there was always hell to pay for choosing what I wanted. I always had to pay the price for making "the wrong choice."

I left my parents' home in my early twenties because I was not in good shape after college. It felt good to leave because it gave me space, yet I also felt bad because I thought that growing up was supposed to be a good thing and wanted to leave on good terms, but that was just not possible. I guess that is one way bullies keep their hooks in. I felt ashamed to go on without them because that was not what I wanted: I did not want to leave them behind. I think I have some survivor's guilt as well as some shame because I felt I failed to find a way to be on good terms with them. Leaving was necessary but terribly hard.

As a result of all this, I find it hard to stand up for myself and I feel both shame and fear at the same time. I get tied up in knots when there is conflict. I have never really felt safe. I have also never felt supported or that anyone had my back, so I try to be as self-reliant as I can. I am much more serious than the people around me, and I'm rarely interested in fun. I was already introverted, but my family life made me more so. I am always afraid of what being different will cost me. To summarize, I am always an outsider, I never fit in, and I have a hard time sticking my neck out.

It was a very tough experience growing up that way because the price you pay to be in the good graces of an authoritarian is to give up your self-respect. If you are not willing to, your life will be hell. The good in us is hidden by authoritarians, which is why they create hopelessness around them. If they can get you to give up your self-respect, undercut your confidence and self-esteem, and destroy your ability to trust, then they will have you as a slave forever, which is what they want.

I remember standing next to my mother once when I was about twelve and realizing that she felt like a shell to me, like there was nothing there. I think that authoritarians want to turn you into an empty shell yourself so that they are not so alone in their emptiness.

JOURNAL PROMPTS

1. Have you experienced your bullying parent as an "empty shell"?

2. What do you think that might signify?

3. Have you lost your desire to "have much of anything"?

Chapter 16

THEFT BY AMPHETAMINES

One thing can lead to another. You are bullied, and you therefore have trouble at school; you are therefore labeled in some way (for instance, as ADHD), and then you are medicated; and a lifetime of mental health interventions, with all of the potentially terrible side effects of those interventions, commences. This is how a direct line can be drawn from bullying to a drug-dominated life. Here is Betty's story.

My dad was the authoritarian in our family. When I was in high school, the only time I really spoke to him during the week or had the chance to speak to him about my ideas was during what was called "our spiritual lesson" each morning at breakfast. I felt like my dad did not know me and that was my only chance to talk to him. I didn't have any time to voice my concerns about my life or about school with him, and my perception was that he didn't have time to hear about who I was as a person or what I needed.

I felt that who I really was didn't matter to him and that he wanted to impose an agenda on me that was not germane to me because he didn't know who I was. I didn't understand why school mattered since it wasn't at all relevant to my life, and I couldn't imagine it being so. This led to problems with my teachers, who told my parents that I was mentally ill with ADD. My parents accepted this view, and I was put on ADD medication for years.

Due to the abysmally poor relationship I had with my father, I consented to taking medication; this was originally an attempt to make myself look better to him as a person, as well as to appear rational and to please him, because I didn't think he thought I was a good person. Taking amphetamines really hurt me and caused a later psychotic break. I will never be the person that I was before I started taking them. I did not like taking them, I did not want to take them, and I did not think I needed them for any reason, yet I took them anyway because my dad was a doctor who constantly made moral judgments, so, I thought he had the authority to be right.

My dad just wanted everything to chug along and happen according to a system or a model because of his confidence in systems and models, and because of his need for convenience. These models were not directly related to a perception of our well-being in the present moment. I think he read some parenting books, and he really valued raising kids who would grow up to be independent in the larger society. But his parenting style was largely about time management and effectiveness. He was implementing what he thought could generally help us based on what he thought had helped him in the past. Mostly he wanted to instill obedience to him in us. This was because he thought he was always right, because he wanted everything to work well and efficiently (with no messes and no inconvenient reality interfering), and because he wanted to raise us with what he thought were moral values based on his religion.

I don't know if I felt wounded; I'm not sure that's the way I would describe it. I understand my dad had good intentions. Instead of seeing myself as having been wounded on an emotional level, what

I feel is that I was physically brain-damaged and developmentally delayed by the pharmacological approach that was employed to achieve my well-being. My psychosis was related to an absence of desperately needed lifestyle interventions, along with being on stimulants on a long-term basis with no relief from taking them. I feel dependent on stimulants to this day in order to function, emotionally and otherwise. The stimulants I take today, which just increase my sense of monotony, remind me of taking Adderall as a kid.

I guess I feel a related sense of emptiness when it comes to my spirituality. I think I would have been able to develop more authentically, spiritually and psychologically, if I hadn't had those interventions. I think I have a different kind of intelligence than what I would have had if I had not been taking amphetamines while my brain was developing as a child. The intelligence I have is an inferior type of intelligence, without the necessary emotional depth to function autonomously and independently in society.

Deprived of the chance to develop my abilities of insight and knowledge organically and deprived of a chance to function as an autonomous, independent and uncompromised being in the world, I have been compromised in my body, my spiritual integrity, and my overall development. The drugs have probably permanently disorganized me. On the ADD medication, I was not able to really feel my emotions, and I became a very cold person, someone with a cool intelligence and the kind of awareness that I still have. This is not my authentic self. The intelligence I have now is just a methed-up, speedy type of intelligence divorced from somatic or bodily awareness and from experiential depth and presence in the world.

It's too bad, I guess, that you have to feel things in order to have a happy and conscious lifestyle. It's too bad that being such an automaton, with my mind divorced from my body, is what my dad and my teachers wanted for me so that I'd succeed in school. I think that the sooner you are able to adapt to the process of feeling (your true emotions) and using them to inform your life, the better off you are. There should be an impact assessment regarding these drugs and how they prevent you from feeling and from having emotions. In my case, I was truly messed up then and I still am. I have permanently lost my grip, and I am still living within the mental health system at the age of twenty-one, just like I was when I was ten.

I am disorganized now and just feel like crap most of the time, and I think it's because of the many drugs I've been on and not getting a chance to learn how to be myself when I was growing up. The impressions I got through the lens of the drug and the drug-induced sense of complete invulnerability, inhumanity, and isolation, both in my relationships with other people and my place in the world, probably permanently handicapped me at that formative stage of childhood. I certainly will never get to experience being a child again—that experience was stolen when I started amphetamines.

JOURNAL PROMPTS

1. Have you entered the mental health system as a consequence of parental bullying?

2. Do you currently live a drug-dominated life?

3. Do you see any options for recovery?

Chapter 17

THEY DOMINATE MY MIND

Your bullying parent may live three thousand miles away. But what if he or she is still in your head and dominating your thoughts? You may see your bullying parent only once or twice a year. But what if he or she is always there, chattering, reprimanding, criticizing, living in a guestroom in your mind? Here is Jed's story.

I have been struggling lately, trying to deal with my parents. I'm fifty-four years old, but you would think that I'm only sixteen years old and that I just got caught drinking a beer. I feel like they are always watching me, always in my head, always on my mind. I can't get rid of them!

Both of my parents were rudely authoritative. When my dad demanded that I needed to make a decision, that meant that I was supposed to do what he wanted me to do. Now, when I need to make a decision, this comes up all over again: that I don't really have a choice in the matter, that the decision is already made, that I'm not really "making a decision" but collapsing in agreement. And I have lots of decisions to make! Each one is like a little skirmish in a bigger war, and I inevitably lose each battle—and, of course, the war.

I have argued with them and hollered at them, both in reality and in my head. I have demanded respect, but nothing ever changes. I only see them once a year, for two weeks in the summer, and yet they dominate my mind when I'm there as well as when I'm at home. I find myself getting into full-blown arguments with my parents, yelling at them here in my room, even though I'm eight hundred miles away from them. I hear their horrible responses and I keep yelling back at them, until finally my wife will walk in and wonder who the hell I'm screaming at.

I never tell her. I'm too embarrassed. I make up some story, maybe that I was yelling at the TV news or cheering a home run or a touchdown. I never tell her that I'm having a full-blown argument with two people who aren't even there. It could be that she knows—I think I scream at them in my sleep, too, and she's probably figured out what's going on. But she hasn't called me on it, so we act like something crazy isn't going on. Of course, it is going on...almost daily.

I stopped talking to my parents about two years ago. I still see them in the summer at the family cabin, but I call my older sister first and make sure that she will be there the same days I will be there. I make sure my brother will show up as well. When the three of us are together, our parents lose their bullying power. But it's more than I should have to do. I should want to see them, just like my kids do. I should enjoy their company, their stories. But I don't. I dread seeing them, they make me nervous and anxious; and so I find ways to get away from them quickly, even though I haven't seen them all year.

I base all my parenting decisions on how I think they would decide—and then I do the opposite. I don't know if I'm raising my kids right, but I do know that I'm not going to do what my parents did! I am especially not going to bring religion into the house. I completely despise religion because my parents are so religious. They reflect no religious or moral values, it's simply the group they belong to, and they don't actually believe a word they're saying. But it's a great weapon. If my kids want to find out about religion, let them do it on their own time—I'm not bringing it into the house.

The bottom line is that my parents still dominate me, and I don't know how. They are forever in my brain. I don't think they are dominating my decisions, because I have this rule of never doing what they would do. But they are dominating my mind. It's some combination of witchcraft and psychological warfare. I think that they're better at what they do than I am at protecting myself. I think they've already won.

JOURNAL PROMPTS

1. Is your bullying parent "in your head?"

2. What new tactic might you try to rid yourself of that voice?

3. What ceremony might you enact to try to rid yourself of that voice?

Chapter 18

WHEN I FELT
STRONG ENOUGH

Victims of parental bullying regularly try to reconcile with the family bully. They may try again and again to have a "normal relationship" with their authoritarian mother or father—and it rarely works, because the family bully has no real interest in such a reconciliation. Here is Patsy's story.

I had a terrible relationship with both my parents, but especially with my mother. She was critical, mean, physically abusive, and really a terror. As a result, I became a passive, frightened, isolated kid. From my childhood years through my teenage years, I had trouble making friends and disliked confrontation, avoiding it if at all possible.

In elementary school, I remember being told I was "boring." I often retreated into an imaginary world in my head. Every day I built my world, invented characters, and escaped into my imagination. Many times, I had superpowers. I could fly, summon fire, and transform into animals at will. I had imaginary friends with powers who would fight evil alongside me. I was their leader. I knew what was best in life, but I never acted any of this out with my body, only in my head.

These stories became as long and vivid as movies or novels. I desperately needed my imagination. It was the one thing I had absolute control over. It was the happiest place where I could be. I didn't know it then, but I was very depressed as a child. I remember always feeling on edge. My chest hurt a lot, and I had trouble sleeping. Even when I was bullied at school, I still dreaded going home, because home was worse. As soon as I came home, I went into my head. The benefit of having had such a rich imagination, I suppose, is that now I love writing fiction.

Once I stopped living with my family, my daydreaming gradually and unconsciously declined, and I started enjoying my life more. Now I only daydream when I actively feel like writing. I also like the world and the people in it a lot more. After I started feeling better, when I felt strong enough, I attempted to "fix" my relationship with my mother by taking her out for lunch once a month. That was truly hard.

There was not much to share with one another since I've left the Catholic church and my mom has no interest in reading my writing. The only times we bonded were over shopping, which really didn't interest me. When enough time had passed that I felt we were on level ground, I gifted her a book of letters, which (unlike my other writings) she did read. Most of the letters praised the good things she had done for me. The last letter in the book I saved to open up my broken heart.

I told her that I felt that religion had ruined our relationship and asked why she hadn't read my book; it had been seven years since I'd finished it. When I met her for one of our lunches, she told me my last letter was "harsh" and that she didn't read my book because "she was angry with me for not marrying in the Catholic church." She also said she had "tried to read it, but didn't really like reading."

I was so furious at having learned all of this that I sent my parents a long email detailing almost everything that was ever done or said to me that had hurt me as a child: from shaking me violently when I didn't know an answer to a math problem, to being told that I "shouldn't rely so much on praise from others," that I was a "b****," and that "the devil was inside me." I broke off communication with them for almost half a year. I had nightmares of yelling at my mother, but soundlessly, because I had no voice. I still have these nightmares.

My husband helped arrange a talk between me and my parents, limiting the time so I would not feel cornered. I originally wanted him to be at my side, but my parents said that they wouldn't speak to me unless I came alone. I accepted their terms, provided that we limited our conversation to no longer than an hour and a half. My dad took "responsibility" for my mom's behavior, blaming himself for not having been there, and said I was "biased" against my mom because she'd had to be the disciplinarian. He went on to explain that he hoped I appreciated the sacrifices they had made to give me a good life as a child. I did not receive any real apology or acknowledgment that how I was treated was wrong.

My mother, who had been silent up until this point, insisted that we should just "forgive and love." At that point, I gave up. I told her "okay," even though I felt neither forgiveness nor love. It was then I realized that I didn't love my mother, and a part of me continues to feel selfish and monstrous for feeling that way. We have get-togethers for birthdays and holidays. I put on a happy face around family members, but deep down I feel like a fraud. The words "I love you, Mom" feel like spikes in my throat. Greeting her with a "Happy Mother's Day" is the hardest of all.

Yet I still buy her cards, I still buy her gifts I think she might like, and I'm often torn between emotions of pride for picking out something nice and shame for feeling like I'm pretending.

In my head, I hear my extended family: "You should forgive your parents. They've done so much for you." Their voices make me angry. I feel like I am constantly performing and playing along, and this is as good as it's going to get between us. It's exhausting. So, I limit my contact to special occasions and try to keep things "light and polite." Unfortunately, I don't like superficial relationships. I like putting everything I have into everything I do, be it my work, my friendships or my love life. It therefore nags at me constantly that my relationship with my parents, especially with my mother, is so far below what I hoped it would be. And I also constantly struggle to get past feeling like the "disappointing," "spoiled," and "ungrateful" daughter.

JOURNAL PROMPTS

1. Have you periodically tried to reconcile with your bullying parent? How has that gone?

2. Do other family members pester you to reconcile with your bullying parent? How do you respond to their pestering?

3. If you were to try again to reconcile, would you try something different this time?

Chapter 19

SO YOU THINK YOU'RE BETTER THAN ME?

Authoritarians see everyone as either patsies or rivals—or both. As a patsy, you are to be used. As a rival, you are to be vanquished. These dynamics play themselves out between an authoritarian parent and his or her child from that child's earliest years. Here is Eleanor's story.

My mother was cold-hearted, compassionless, unbearably loud, always angry...and always right. It seemed that her only real interest in her daughters was that we were seen and not heard and that we did well in school so that she could take credit for our accomplishments. She ruled us with an iron hand.

We were living in Europe at that time; my father was in the service. I don't know what I was doing to provoke it, but when I was about nine years old a viciously hard slap came out of nowhere, landing on my right cheek. I remember my shock at the stinging pain and mother's raging words, calling me a god-damned stupid ass. I know I was beaten, but I don't remember much about it.

What I do know is that her slaps and beatings succeeded in silencing me. She could actually strike the words from my mouth and the thoughts from my mind. As an introverted, quiet child, I learned not to speak up, not to ask for help, and not to assert myself. I hated myself for being, as she called me, "stupid," "a selfish brat," and "useless."

Through the years, when there were difficult circumstances in school or in my relationships, I couldn't think clearly enough to figure out how I felt or find the words to stand up for myself. I always felt there was something terribly wrong with me. To this day, it feels as if there is damage caused by my upbringing. I often experience heightened anxiety; at times, I find myself near panic if I have to speak to a group of people, and any criticism and I become undone. All I can say is, it has not been an easy life.

It feels that embedded in my psyche is the notion that I will receive negative feedback for whatever choices I make. There is always the possibility that others might be offended by my choice. As a sixty-eight-year-old retired woman, it felt a bit outrageous for me to be applying for an MFA degree. I didn't tell anyone because I didn't want to hear anyone's opinion about it. I felt I was, in some way, being foolish or arrogant, and I didn't want to be judged as trying to be "better than" the other artists I know.

My efforts to apply to the MFA program brought back bad memories of how my mother treated me when I applied for college back in 1970. Her response was, "So, you think that you're better than me?" It was such a strange response, one that I still can't really understand. Why was I her rival? Why was I her competition? I was just her little girl, not someone brought onto this earth as a reproach to her and a constant reminder of what she wasn't and all that she hadn't done. I am still struck by the sheer unfairness of her making me her rival.

When, to my surprise, I was accepted for the MFA program, I told a friend of mine the good news, and she responded, "Why on earth would you do that? Why don't you just enjoy your retirement?" I wish

I could have said, "*I am* enjoying my retirement," or "I'm committed to lifelong learning," or any one of the myriad responses that would have conveyed my right to be making a decision for myself. Instead, it was like that cruel slap across the face, coming out of nowhere, blotting out my words and thoughts, just like when I was a kid.

It is always surprising to me that people can be so bold to judge others for their choices. Because of my experience growing up, I would never do that to someone else. I do not need to play the game of thinking that everyone else is wrong, bad, misguided, stupid, an enemy, an ass...all the things that my mother piled on me. I may still be too meek and too often silenced, but I do not need to be my mother.

JOURNAL PROMPTS

1. Did your bullying parent effectively silence you?

2. Do you fear the opinions of others?

3. Is there something you would like to say to someone whose opinion you fear?

Chapter 20

SNAPSHOTS OF CONSEQUENCES

Family bullies are harming their children. If the preceding stories didn't prove that, common sense does. What are the lifelong negative consequences? They are exactly what you might suppose: despair, anxiety, low self-esteem, a damaged self-image, fearfulness, relationship difficulties, addictions, an inability to concentrate or to think clearly, grief, suicidal thoughts, and more.

Virtually all of the respondents to my Authoritarian Wound Questionnaire reported as one consequence of authoritarian wounding a heightened sense of anxiety. This anxiety manifests itself in all sorts of ways; it manifests as nausea, confusion, panic attacks, phobic reactions, sweats, forgetfulness, dissociative episodes, chronic worries, unproductive obsessions, impulsivity, powerful compulsions, procrastination, passive-aggressive behaviors, and every manner of physical and mental distress you can imagine.

Another set of consequences involves the body. No one doubts that there is a mind/body connection. However, people find it harder to accept that past trauma and present trauma can produce physical illness. We hate to think that we've opened ourselves up to respiratory problems, digestive problems, other physical ailments and medical conditions, and even chronically poor health in general because of the way our mind works, because of the way our personality has formed, and because of the harm done to us. But that's exactly what a mind/body connection implies: Our mental, emotional, and psychological states affect our physical health.

Another common consequence is relationship mayhem. Many of the respondents to my Authoritarian Wound Questionnaire who experienced authoritarian wounding in childhood went on to pick an authoritarian mate. This "repetition compulsion" is hard to understand, and the explanations that respondents tended to give, for instance, that they choose an authoritarian mate because it "felt familiar," don't feel like the whole story. Whatever the psychological reasons for this "repetition compulsion," it occurs with regularity.

Here are half a dozen snapshots of the consequences of being bullied by a parent. I could have presented a much larger number of snapshots, but let's let these six suffice.

Jeanette explained: "I have chronic anxiety around the clock, 24/7. Most days I am at a level four or five out of ten. Some days it's higher and some days it's lower, but it is always there, and I can *never* fully relax. When the anxiety becomes really bad, I sometimes slide into a depression, believing something is wrong with me and that I am too flawed. I then spiral down to wanting to give up because I struggle so much every day. This leads to suicidal thoughts."

Marcia shared: "For a long time, I had no sense of self or identity, no idea who I was, no idea what I wanted in life nor who I wanted to be. I floated along, going to college and getting a job, living overseas because my boyfriend suggested it, doing things because others wanted it or because it was 'the next step.' I was an expert at molding myself into what others wanted me to be, and this left me prone to falling for a narcissist, whom I married and was with for fifteen years."

Lydia explained: "My older sister dropped out of high school, ran away from home, and became addicted to drugs and alcohol. I didn't see her for a very long time. Only recently have we begun talking to each other again, and I'm learning that she has the exact same feelings as me, the exact same mental disorders, and cites the exact same reason, our mother. Though she's ten years older than me, and I barely remember living with her because I was six years old when she left our house, she tells me stories of living with my mother that sound so familiar that I cry."

Sandra shared: "In the early years of my marriage (which is presently very happy), talking to my husband about anything we had a disagreement on was difficult for me. I often felt (rightly or wrongly) as if my opinion was not being listened to or taken seriously, which led to my anger becoming explosive, just like my mother's. I would then feel guilty about my behavior and withdraw emotionally, falling into a deep depression. We would make up and go through a nice period until we had a disagreement, and then the cycle would repeat itself."

Robert explained: "I don't even know where to begin. I have developed anxiety and depression, which I've had for as long as I can remember. I can't maintain close intimate relationships—I always turn cold and distant and hateful. I am pretty much a narcissist like my father. I have no self-confidence, I hide from the world, I have drug problems now, sex addiction problems, I don't take care of my health whatsoever, and quite frankly, I don't care enough about myself to even come up with a reason why I should do healthy things."

Janet shared: "I think that the following are among the consequences of growing up with an authoritarian dad. One is an overwhelming sense of guilt when I put my own needs first. A second is my inability to relate to my siblings without casting on them the exact same judgments my dad levelled on them. For example, my sister was adopted, and it was quite clear that my dad didn't really want her. I've only realized in the past couple of years, since my brother died and since my sister and I have both ended our relationship with our dad, that I cast judgments on her and subtle rejections that I'd picked up from him."

Our experiences matter. Our experiences produce consequences. Our experiences affect us, they shape us, and, if they are adverse, they harm us.

JOURNAL PROMPTS

1. How were you affected by parental bullying? What were the consequences?

2. Are you attracted to people with the same qualities and characteristics as your parental bully?

3. Are you aware of physical consequences that you can attribute to the harm done to you?

Chapter 21

EIGHT TRUTHS

Here are eight truths to hold onto as we move toward Part II of our examination of family bullies. In Part II, I'll describe a toolkit of tactics and strategies for healing and survival. Here, take in these eight truths (and you may want to think about them and do some writing):

TRUTH 1. THIS REALLY HAPPENED (YOU WEREN'T CRAZY)

We can almost believe that what happened to us didn't happen to us, maybe because we did a lot of dissociating, maybe because other people saw the authoritarian in a different light, maybe because we wished so hard that it wasn't true or that bad, or for some other reason. But it did happen.

Please try your hand at one or more of the following journal prompts, either on the computer or writing in your favorite journal. Note that they are written from your point of view:

1. What exactly went on? Let me pick one experience that still deeply affects me and try to describe it as carefully as I can. I do want to know for certain that what I believe went on actually did go on.

2. I want to think a little bit about how it might be to remember some of those terrible experiences without having to re-experience them and without having to be flooded with bad feelings. Can I see a way to do that?

3. I have thought for a long time that I must be a little crazy to believe that such awful things could possibly have gone on. But they did happen. So, how can I let go of that feeling that I was "a little crazy" for believing what it turns out was completely appropriate to believe?

TRUTH 2. YOU DIDN'T HAVE A CHOICE (YOU DIDN'T CHOOSE IT)

If your experience of dealing with an authoritarian happened in childhood, it should be clear to you that you didn't choose to experience that wounding. But as clear as that truth may be, it's still easy to feel complicit or as if you deserved what happened to you, maybe because you weren't "perfect." Now is a good moment to get clear on the fact that you didn't choose to be abused by that parental bully.

Please pick one or more of the following prompts to write on:

1. Is there some part of me that still thinks that I did choose my situation? How can I still be thinking that? And what can I do to stop thinking that?

2. If I'm still dealing with an authoritarian today, do I have new choices to make? Do I need to make different choices?

3. Because I didn't have any choice in the matter growing up, I think I may have gotten it into my head that I'm not entitled to make strong choices or maybe that I'm not equal to choosing. I think I'd like to do some reflecting on that possibility.

TRUTH 3. YOU DIDN'T HAVE ALLIES (YOU HAD TO GO IT ALONE)

It is hard to overestimate the extent to which you had to go it alone. Authoritarians can't function if everyone around them says, "No!" For the authoritarian to bully others, those others must be staying silent, not fighting back, tacitly accepting the situation, or even defending the authoritarian. Maybe you were lucky to have an ally in an aunt, a sibling, or someone else, but basically you had to go it alone—the proof is that no one ever successfully stopped the bully's behavior.

Please pick one or more of the following prompts to write on:

1. Did I have any real allies during those bad times, or didn't I? What was the exact nature of my situation with respect to allies and/or a lack of external support?

2. If I did have a real ally during those times and he or she is still living, do I want to reach out and say something to him or her?

Do I possibly want to say something to him or her, even if he or she is deceased?

3. I wonder, what were the consequences of having had to go it alone? Did that make me independent or dependent? Did it make me love solitude or recoil from solitude? Let me do a little writing and tease out those consequences.

TRUTH 4. YOU DIDN'T HAVE POWER (YOU COULDN'T FIGHT BACK)

Grown-ups possess all the power. Children can dream and fantasize about being powerful and engage in small acts of rebellion, but they are essentially powerless in the face of adult abuse. This true powerlessness can produce lifelong feelings of powerlessness, even though you are now an adult with all the powers of an adult.

Please pick one or more of the following prompts to write on:

1. I want to think clearly about the ways in which I was powerless in those terrible times, primarily for the sake of making absolutely certain that I do not blame myself for not taking actions that were just not available to me.

2. How would I describe the power I now possess? Surely, I do possess some adult powers! How would I describe them? And how do I use them?

3. What would it take to transform myself into a "real-life superhero"? And what would I be able to accomplish then?

TRUTH 5. YOU COULDN'T POSSIBLY HAVE UNDERSTOOD (HOW COULD YOU?)

You may blame yourself for not understanding what was going on, for having been too innocent, for missing what was right in front of your nose. But how could you possibly have understood? Feeling that something was seriously wrong and fully understanding the complicated dynamics of the authoritarian personality are two different things. Really, how could you have understood?

Please pick one or more of the following prompts to write on:

1. What do I understand now that I couldn't possibly have understood back then?

2. What intuitions and intimations that I had back then about my situation and about what was going on were actually accurate? Did I perhaps have some understanding of the situation that I couldn't quite access then?

3. Is there something to forgive or to heal with regard to what I didn't know back then?

TRUTH 6. YOU WERE GENUINELY AFRAID (OF COURSE YOU FELT SCARED)

Authoritarians scare us. You may have spent much of your childhood terrified. Of course you were afraid. The question to grapple with now is, do you still have to be afraid today?

Please pick one or more of the following prompts to write on:

1. I want to remember what it was like to be frightened as a child so as to validate that experience. I am going to go back in memory, remember what I felt, and honor that I had those terrible experiences. But I am going to go back very carefully.

2. I know that I've lived in a fearful way and that I've been scared a lot in life. What can I do to feel safer now?

3. I want to live differently. How can I live more bravely? What would such a life look like?

TRUTH 7. HEALING IS POSSIBLE (IN PART, THROUGH WRITING)

Naturally enough, you may have gotten into the habit of thinking that nothing much can change in life, including, perhaps especially, your own personality. But healing, change, and growth really are possible. You can use your reflective writing practice to help you make the changes that you identify ought to be made.

Please pick one or more of the following prompts to write on:

1. I think I'd like to describe a daily practice that will serve me as I try to shed the psychological and emotional baggage of the past.

2. I want to create a firm yet gentle action plan that supports my intention to heal, grow, and live well.

3. I want to write about a better, brighter future, one where I feel less burdened by the past and more optimistic and passionate about the future. Let me write about that.

TRUTH 8. THE STRENGTHS YOU BRING

To say that you were wounded by the authoritarians in your life isn't to speak metaphorically. Something in you was literally injured. Maybe it was your willingness or your ability to deal with conflict. Maybe it was your self-image, your self-esteem, or your self-trust. Maybe it was your ability to trust others or to care deeply about others. The list of possible injuries is long. But you also have many strengths—many!

JOURNAL PROMPTS

1. Which of these truths strikes you as most important to think about?

2. Do any of these truths not seem self-evident to you?

3. What thoughts and feelings has thinking about these truths conjured up in you?

Part II

TOOLS AND
TACTICS

Chapter 22

CREATE PHYSICAL SEPARATION AND LIMIT CONTACT

Adult survivors of authoritarian wounding and family bullying regularly report that only physical separation between them and the authoritarian in question allowed them to feel safe and provided them with the opportunity to heal. And the wider the separation, the better. Of all of my research findings, this is the most robust. Adult survivors reported physical separation as their number one safety and survival strategy.

Adam shared the following: "I had a good job offer locally and a second-best job offer clear across the country. But my decision was actually a no-brainer. If I had stayed within shouting distance of my abusive mom, I would have been eaten alive. She would have guilt-tripped me ten times a day about not visiting her, about not running errands she needed run, about not making repairs around the house, about not playing cards with her, about not bringing her treats, about not driving her wherever she wanted to go. How can you put a price on not having to live that way? That second-best offer looked like a dream come true, because it got me three thousand miles away from my mother."

Marj explained: "We are what is euphemistically called a 'close' family. They make movies about families like ours, where everyone is loud, laughing, passing plates around a huge dining room table, joking around, having a whale of a good time. That's the movie version. Our real-life version is that every family member has his or her claws and fangs out. If you're overweight, you'll hear about it. If you're out of work, you'll hear about it. If your boyfriend left you, you'll hear about it. Everybody is mean to everybody else. And still, the unwritten code is that we're supposed to live near each other, like within half a mile—and to move farther away is to betray the family. I moved two miles away, and I never heard the end of it. So, I thought, in for a nickel, in for a dollar—and moved across the state. It was the smartest move I've ever made."

In your case, you may still be living with your bullying parent, or you may have returned to live with your bullying parent again, perhaps because your parent has become ill or infirm. For you, then, complete physical separation isn't possible. The smart question for you to pose in that situation is, "What's the least amount of contact I can have with my mom?" or "How can I stay out of my dad's way most of the time?" If you can't orchestrate complete physical separation, limiting contact is the next strategy to try.

What might it look like to limit contact? Amelia explained, "I moved back into the family house to take care of my mother when none of my siblings were willing to even lend a hand. I hated that I guilt-tripped myself into doing that, but I also loved my mother, so it was a complicated moment. But what I did was only see my mother when I absolutely had to. I was otherwise really unavailable. I chose a room in the house far away from my mother, I went out a lot, and, most importantly, I made it clear to myself that I didn't need to 'keep her company'—because 'keeping her company' was inevitably toxic."

John has a different story: "My dad is ill, and his house is falling apart. That house is our inheritance. Getting a good price for it when the time comes matters to my brother, my sister, and me. Because I have the skills, it's on my shoulders to make the repairs that the house needs. To call in a contractor and subs would cost an arm and a leg. So, I do the work—which means that I see my drunken father far too often. But I know his routine. I know when he's awake and itching for a fight, and when he's passed out. It's going to take longer to make the repairs if I only show up when he's not up and trying to start something—but that will save me my sanity. Better that the repairs go at a snail's pace than that I lose my mind—or my temper."

However you decide to play it, there are bound to be trade-offs. By moving a thousand miles away, you may create a safe distance between you and your bullying mother or father, but at the same time, you may dramatically reduce the time you can spend with your sister and your nieces, who you'll be leaving behind. Plus, you may feel guilty for leaving your sister and her children "alone" with your bullying parent. That isn't going to feel good. But you must consider your own mental and physical well-being, your own safety needs, and your own life path. There may be real costs to leaving, but greater costs to staying.

We'll give Larry the last word on this. He explained, "I find it impossible to deal with my father. His politics and his attitudes disgust me, his scapegoating is nonstop, the way he bullies my mom is unbearable to witness, and he's on the edge of violence all the time. It takes all of about two minutes before we're at it. Finally, my wife laid down the law. It was either leave the area or she would leave me. At first, I made up all sorts of excuses about why we couldn't leave—it kind of amazed me that I was doing that, but I was. Something had a hold on me. But after one completely terrible interaction at my dad's house, I finally threw in the towel. Whatever I was still clinging to, whatever secret hope I was still harboring, that was finally that. We moved very far away—and that move was absolutely necessary."

JOURNAL PROMPTS

1. Is physical separation from the parental bully in your life possible? If it is possible, should you create that distance?

2. If physical separation isn't possible, is limited contact possible?

3. What might it look like to limit contact?

Chapter 23

CREATE PSYCHOLOGICAL SEPARATION

You may need to get the parental bully in your family out of your life through physical distancing and limited contact. But if he or she is still on your mind, you haven't created enough separation. You need to keep that parental bully out of your mind. Of course, there are times when you are bound to think about your father or your mother and times when it is necessary to think about them. But you do not want to let them hound you—you do not want to give them permanent seats in the room that is your mind.

This is much easier to say than to do. Victims may still love their parents, or feel that they ought to love them. They may find themselves pressured by other family members to continue to deal with their parents, thus preventing psychological and emotional separation. And just as a matter of habit, they may think about their parents—their grievances against their parents, the harm done to them by their parents, and at times revenge fantasies where they get even with their parents—far too often.

What does this enmeshment and inner torture sound like? Mark put it this way: "Both of my parents have been dead for more than ten years, and I'm still not free of them. I still rage at them internally; I keep telling them what they did to me; they keep denying it and shaming me; and all of this is going on in my own head. This is all my own doing now. Meditation hasn't helped; cognitive therapy hasn't helped. I feel like I need some kind of surgery. The only thing that helps is drugs—and I know that can't be the right answer. Being a drug addict can't be the answer."

Mary Jo described her situation this way:

> I grew up in the rust belt in a small town. Everyone knew everyone, and things like high school football and homecoming queens and babysitting and going to the reservoir meant the world to us—they made up our world. But inside my house, it was not the American dream. We were on top of each other, and my mother couldn't cope. My father never wanted children, and he expressed his resentment about that by demanding a kind of military discipline that made no sense and that probably wasn't really him. Well, whether it really was him or really wasn't him, he bullied us all, some of us kids more than others.
>
> For a period of time, when I went away to college and began making my way in the world, I didn't think about them much. I had a ton of other things on my mind. But as life would have it, they moved to San Diego, and I also moved there for work, but also to be "closer to them." I thought that was what I wanted and what they wanted. But then, suddenly, they were on my mind all the time, even though I only saw them once a week for dinner. I couldn't stop thinking about them, about what it was like in our house growing up, about how messed up some of my siblings were, about the great discrepancy

between how my parents looked now—decent enough—and how they were back then.

My work provided therapy, which didn't work, because my therapist wanted to label me with depression and anxiety and put me on medication, and I knew that wasn't what I needed. I tried all sorts of practices, this kind of meditation or that kind of meditation, and they worked somewhat, they were positive in their own right, but they didn't help with the constant obsessing. Talking to my siblings didn't help—they were so full of hatred and resentment that talking to them just made me upset. Then I found something that helped a lot—hiking.

I began hiking Oak Canyon, Seven Bridge Walk, Grinding Rocks, Annie's Canyon, and the other great hiking trails that San Diego County has to offer. When I was out hiking, my mind would get completely quiet. But the benefits also lasted. If I did a good hike on a Saturday morning, I might spend the whole day not thinking about my parents once. I have no idea why that worked, but it was a complete blessing that it did. It isn't fanciful to say that those hikes saved my life. They aren't a complete answer—but, after all, what could be? What could possibly be a complete answer to the question, "How can you get your parents out of your head?"

You may never quite be able to get your parents out of your head, but that's the high-bar goal we're after. We'll look at two methods for doing that over the next two chapters: first, by learning to "think thoughts that serve you;" and second, by redesigning your mind so that your parents are denied comfortable permanent residence there. Let's continue the process of escorting the bully in your life out of your head. A key to your safety—and maybe even to your very survival—is creating the psychological separation you need between you and the bully in your mind. Let's continue.

JOURNAL PROMPTS

1. Is your parental bully on your mind a lot? Is this the case even if he or she is deceased?

2. What, if anything, do you try to do to get him or her out of your mind?

3. Any thoughts about what new strategies you might like to try so as to rid yourself of that destructive noise?

Chapter 24

PRACTICE RIGHT THINKING

In the second half of this book, we'll be looking at an array of tools and tactics that you can employ to deal with past bullying, the leftovers of which exist in the mind, in the body, and in our very personality. We'll also be looking at tactics for dealing with current bullying, if you still live with your parents; and techniques for dealing with the intermittent bullying that occurs if you maintain contact with your bullying parent. One crucial tactic is a core cognitive one: practicing right thinking. No practice is more important. Trauma causes us to think thoughts that do not serve us. Because we've been harmed, because the world feels scary and uninviting, because our self-image has been tarnished, we may begin to think thoughts like "I can't succeed," and "I have no chance," and "Who cares anyway?" and "What's the point?" These and similar thoughts rob us of our power, prevent us from living our life purposes, and do us no good at all.

No skill is more important than learning to think thoughts that serve you. By thinking thoughts that serve you, you help rid your system of the toxic effects of trauma. The practice of thinking thoughts that serve you is made up of two steps. First, when you think a thought that doesn't serve you, you notice what you just said to yourself and instantly replace it with a thought that better serves you.

For instance, you might suddenly think, "I have no chance in life," which might be followed by a mood swing into despair or lead to a behavior like pouring yourself a double Scotch or driving recklessly, looking for an accident. If you are practicing the skill of right thinking, the instant you hear yourself say, "I have no chance in life," you would demand of yourself that you say, "No, that thought doesn't serve me!"

Then, second, you would think a thought that better serves you, for instance a thought like, "I am adamant about succeeding," or "I absolutely do have a chance!" Notice that you are saying "That thought doesn't serve me," rather than "That thought isn't true." This is a huge shift and one that prevents you from getting hijacked by true thoughts that, while true, don't serve you.

Thus, the second step of this two-step strategy is to actively think thoughts that *do* serve you. Step one was to notice that you were thinking a thought that didn't serve you and to say no to it. Step two is to choose to think a thought that does serve you. Of course, you would want to think thoughts that serve you even if an unwanted thought hadn't preceded it. That is, you are after the high-bar result of always thinking thoughts that serve you.

Let doing this become a habit and a practice. You might, for example, wake up each morning and say to yourself, "I am living my life purposes today." That is a thought that serves you. You might follow that thought with thoughts like, "I'm practicing calmness today," and "I'm loving my children today," i.e., more thoughts that serve you. In this way, by choosing the thoughts you intend to think and by then thinking them in an intentional way, you begin to extinguish thoughts that haven't been serving you, and in the process, you do yourself a world of good.

Sometimes the thoughts that aren't serving us are so muffled that we don't quite understand them, although we hear them just enough to upset ourselves. Or they may pass by so quickly that we don't quite realize that we just had a suspect thought, though now our mood has worsened or we suddenly feel unmotivated. Because both of these aspects of thinking regularly derail us—those whispered thoughts that we don't quite hear and those rapid thoughts that zip on by and leave a terrible residue—we have to learn to hear those muffled ones and register those quick ones. Only if we hear them and register them can we dispute them and replace them with thoughts that do serve us.

You can see that the practice of right thinking is real work. You need to be disputing thoughts that don't serve you the instant they bubble up. You need to be introducing thoughts that do serve you via the regular practice of right thinking. You need to be listening for those terrible almost-silent thoughts and noticing those painful fleeting ones. This is rather a full-time job, because we are always thinking thoughts and those thoughts need to be monitored. One stray thought can trigger a flood of emotions or a dark mood, which is why real vigilance is required.

No skill better helps us deal with current bullying and heal the trauma of past bullying than this right thinking. If you are currently being bullied and you hear yourself think, "I hate myself," "I hate my life," or "I can't take this anymore," you would, if your right thinking practice is in place, shake your head, counter that thought with, "No, you are not a thought that serves me," and proceed to think a thought that does serve you, like, "I am not the problem," "I must find some allies," or "I need to find a place to go after school." Right thinking is not a complete solution—we have many more tools and tactics to discuss—but it is an important one, one that will serve you in every aspect of your experience your whole life long.

JOURNAL PROMPTS

1. Describe this two-step process in your own words.

2. What are some characteristic thoughts that you know aren't serving you?

3. Pick one or two of these thoughts. The next time you hear them, what do you want to say to yourself instead?

Chapter 25

REDESIGN YOUR MIND

It is a rich metaphor to say that we experience our mind as a room where we spend our time. For each of us, that room has a particular, idiosyncratic feel to it. For some, it is a claustrophobic place very much like a prison. For others, it is a chaotic place where no rest or peace is possible. For some—unfortunately, the minority—it is a welcoming place filled with sunlight and warm breezes. What sort of "room" is your mind?

If you've been traumatized, then trauma has found its way into that room. It may inhabit it as a permanent sandstorm, making it hard and maybe even impossible to think, muse, or relax in your own skin. It may inhabit your mind as constant chatter, as a noisy parrot in a prominent cage that keeps squawking out thoughts that don't serve you. It may inhabit your mind as a bed of nails, as a painful surface that makes you wince and sometimes even scream as you try to walk across it or rest on it.

Many things can help heal trauma. One of those many things is among the most important—and it is one that we have direct control over. That is getting a grip on your own mind. Philosophers from Marcus Aurelius to the Buddha have stated the extent to which that is a top priority. Cognitive-behavioral therapy is the modern way that this age-old message is delivered. Almost everyone knows a little bit about cognitive-behavioral therapy and many people have worked with a CB therapist. Why is CBT so popular, so much so that CBT is the primary therapy provided by the United Kingdom's National Health Service? Because its central message is indubitably true: You are what you think.

However, the ways that you are invited to get a grip on your mind, whether those invitations come from traditions like Stoicism or Buddhism or from cognitive-behavioral therapists, are a bit on the dull side and may strike us as unimaginative. Sit there and meditate? Block a thought and substitute another thought? How playful or inspired is that? As a smart, creative, imaginative person, you deserve something a little more daring and interesting. How about the idea of redesigning and redecorating the room that is your mind?

Let's call the experience of visiting that room that is your mind and spending time there *indwelling*. Indwelling can be unhealthy, for instance, when you spend your time pestering yourself, bad-mouthing yourself, and so on. Or it can be healthy, when you think thoughts that serve you, update your plans so that they match your lived experience, and so on. The sort of indwelling we're after is healthy indwelling. Healthy indwelling heals.

Can you cultivate a mindful, aware indwelling style so that the time you spend in that room that is your mind stops feeling painful? You can if you try. Visualize that room. Take an inventory of its contents. Make some decisions about how you'd like to redesign it and redecorate it. What pops to mind?

Maybe you'd like to add windows that let in a breeze. Perhaps you'd like to replace that bed of nails with a comfy armchair. Maybe you'd like to remove that parrot cage and let that squawking parrot go free. Play with this metaphor and enjoy it. Visit the room that is your mind, while holding healthier indwelling as your goal, and call on your excellent redecorating skills to remodel, refresh, and renew that indwelling space.

Let's focus on that bed of nails. I bet that right now there is a pain-inducing bed of nails prominently positioned in the middle of your mindroom. It's the bed of nails you've installed to make yourself remember *at all times* that you've failed yourself. It's there to punish you for mangling your life. Isn't part of you certain that you deserve that bed of nails, that you should writhe in pain, that piercing yourself on those sharp metal points is the only way to expiate your guilt?

Let's get rid of it! *Right now, visualize getting rid of it.* Call in the haulers and get it the heck out of there. Watch the haulers leave with it. Pay them a little extra to destroy it so that no one else finds it and thinks that they deserve it. Tip the haulers handsomely and thank them profusely. They are carrying out the thing that has harmed you the most, your enduring self-indictment. It is time to sign your pardon. That bed of nails is, and has always been, cruel if not unusual punishment.

Okay! It's been hauled away. Next, go online in your mind's eye and buy yourself exactly the easy chair that you've never permitted yourself. Make sure it's comfortable! Skip that chair-as-art that was never meant to sit on. Get something comfy. You want an easy chair that is genuinely easy to relax in because that ease is going to translate into better living. Take your time shopping!

Picture where you'll place your easy chair in your mindroom. Point the movers to exactly where you want it positioned. Then sit! Do you deserve that easy chair? Of course, you do. Do you deserve it even though you've made a hash of this and a mash of that? Of course, you do. Do you deserve it even though you were to blame for that terrible A, even though you were the cause of that horrible B, and even though you didn't help when it came to that awful C? Of course, you do. By purchasing it and by sitting in it, you are announcing that you are human, and that, warts and all, you deserve some ease.

Your easy chair is your place for relaxation, rejuvenation, daydreams, bursts of imagination, forgiveness, hard thinking, renewed hope, and everything else better done in an easy chair than on a bed of nails. No doubt you agree; and yet it may prove hard to part with your bed of nails. It exists in your mind because for the longest time you've been certain that you deserve it. Part of you is positive that you ought to punish yourself for all those messes, mistakes, and missteps. It's time to get rid of it!

When you form an intention, like replacing that bed of nails with an easy chair, there are two excellent additional steps to take besides visualizing the change. One is to begin to actively think thoughts that support that intention, as we discussed in the last chapter. Here, for example, are five thoughts that support that intention:

1. "No bed of nails for me!"

2. "I love my easy chair!"

3. "I am worthy."

4. "Lightness and ease."

5. "I am becoming more self-friendly."

Imagine entering your mindroom, throwing open the windows, and enjoying the soft breeze, exclaiming, "I love my easy chair!" and sitting down in your easy chair to think, dream, imagine, or remember. Isn't that the ticket!

Second, you can support an intention by engaging in new behaviors. For example, here are five behaviors that support your intention to replace your usual self-pestering with a new self-friendly lightness and ease.

1. Begin to notice which of your behaviors seem to come from a self-unfriendly place. To begin with, just notice.

2. Pick one behavior that looks to be coming from that self-unfriendly place. Give yourself the following instruction: "The next time I'm about to behave in that way, I'm going to visit my mindroom, get comfy in my easy chair, and see if that makes a difference."

3. When you feel yourself about to behave in that self-unfriendly way, visualize that bed of nails being hauled away. Wave goodbye to it. See if that makes a difference.

4. Repeat this process with another behavior that looks to be coming from that same self-unfriendly place.

5. Continue the process of identifying self-unfriendly behaviors and countering each with those two visualizations of the bed of nails being hauled away and of you comfy in your easy chair.

Nothing is more important to change than the ways that we diminish, derail, defeat, and inflict pain on ourselves. Redesigning your mind can help you make that change. It's as easy as shutting your eyes and visualizing.

JOURNAL PROMPTS

1. Describe "redesigning your mind" in your own words.

2. Picture the room that is your mind. How would you like to redesign it and redecorate it?

3. Actually redesign it. Does your experience of indwelling feel any different?

Chapter 26

GROW YOUR STRENGTH

It takes strength to deal with the parental bully in your life. It takes strength to create physical and psychological distance, to limit contact, to protect yourself and keep yourself safe, to enlist allies, and to speak up—every action, every practice, every step of the way requires strength. I've found that inviting clients to manifest new strength resonates with them. They may not feel equal to the task, but the idea makes sense to them.

Strength is required. Being criticized over and over again is more wearing than a long march. Feeling abandoned, misunderstood, or rejected is harder on the system than climbing a mountain. We need great strength to say what we mean to say, if saying what we mean feels threatening and comes with the danger of retaliation. We need great strength to deal with someone who envies our success, who snickers at our life choices, or who requires our constant attention. All of that requires strength.

This is not a strength that we can acquire in the gym, though being healthy and fit is certainly a good thing. This is an internal fortitude that we must muster and manifest. This looks like us instantly disputing self-talk like "I can't do that" with a firm "Yes, I can!" When I work with clients, we spend a lot of time focusing on manifesting this strength. One of the ways we do that is by rehearsing and role-playing. Often what's required before a person can manifest her strength is rehearsing what she intends to say, visualizing the interaction in all its details, and picturing consequences.

What does manifesting strength look like? One client hated it that her husband would not follow through on a certain "simple" household project. Their downstairs bathroom needed a new toilet, and her husband had gotten as far as removing the old toilet, then set it down in the living room and stopped there.

That old toilet was now sitting in her living room and had sat there for months. Not only was it an eyesore, and not only did it prevent her from socializing in her own home—it was living proof of the difficulties she was having in her marriage as well as a reproach that seemed to scream at her, "You are so weak!"

It took all her strength to give her husband the ultimatum that this toilet-in-the-living-room thing was a marriage deal-breaker. Even with that ultimatum, he still took his own sweet time finishing the downstairs bathroom remodel—but at least a day did come when that old toilet finally left the living room.

Another client found that she was being held hostage by her mother's will. She had given over her life to caretaking her aged mother, and each time she tried to discuss the possibility that some other arrangement had to be made so that she, the daughter, could have a life, her mother would threaten to remove her from her will.

This threat had worked for many years. It took us some time to discern what concrete "strength" she needed to muster in order to free herself from the grip of that dangled legacy. Finally, we came upon it: she needed to buy a plane ticket to the place where she intended to relocate. With that ticket in hand, she was able to have the conversation with her mother that she had needed to have for so long, one that she now felt strong enough to engage in no matter what her mother threatened about the will.

A third client needed to find the strength to continue with her writing career even though her husband had grown very envious of her success. He craved the income she produced but also belittled her efforts, which had caused her to become blocked and stop writing. She came to me not understanding why she wasn't writing, given that she loved writing, felt connected to her current writing project, and had readers waiting for her next book. It quickly became clear that her husband's passive-aggressive attitude toward her success had somehow crept into her psyche and caused her to block.

In her case, the strength that she had to muster was the not inconsiderable strength it takes to live with a passive-aggressive mate. She had to tune him out, she had to call him on his behaviors (like filling up her writing study with "things that we don't have room for in the garage"), and she had to speak to him clearly and directly about not belittling her readers, her genre, or her efforts.

A fourth client had to find the strength to send her teenager away to a therapeutic wilderness camp despite his loud unwillingness to go. For several years he'd been declining, doing progressively more poorly in school, picking up a drug and alcohol habit, and finally, as a last straw, dealing drugs. Now the law had gotten involved—and even that drama did not seem to wake her son up to his predicament.

My client held this wilderness camp as her last hope, and it took mustering all her strength to demand that he go, despite his violent protestations and self-harm threats. In fact, the wilderness camp experience seemed to turn his life around—which is often the sort of blessing a person receives when she is able to manifest her strength within her troubled family.

Very often, we live as a weakened version of ourselves because life has beaten us down, because we've failed too many times and no longer trust ourselves to succeed, because we have trouble holding a clear vision of our life purposes and our most important intentions, or for other reasons. Of course, one of those reasons will be the authoritarian wounding we've experienced. I hope that the above examples give you a taste of what "working on strength" might look like.

Theresa explained:

> I found myself in the following odd situation. My father seemed to have "gotten better" and had pretty much stopped bullying me, criticizing me, and belittling my efforts. He even praised some brownies I brought over, without any left-handed slap at them. I'd never experienced that before. I felt some compassion well up in me, and I could sense that I was about to say something really dangerous, like, "Maybe we could take that trip to Florida together," a trip we'd talked about once or twice to visit my aunt, my father's sister. I could feel saying that right on the tip of my tongue.
>
> But I found the strength not to speak. I so wanted to come from a "good girl" place, to let him off the hook for everything, to turn a blind eye to how that trip would really go, and just embrace my "new" dad. It took so much real strength not to speak! It was like holding back a tidal wave. And I knew that I had better get out of there—that I only had so much strength and that the dike holding back that tidal wave might break. I stayed away for several weeks—that took its own kind of

strength. "Staying on guard" is a funny kind of strength, but absolutely what was required.

You build your muscles through daily exercise and by spending real time at the gym. Building the sort of strength that we've been discussing requires the same daily practice. There is no gym to go to—the gym is life. Practice your new strength out in the world, in your dealings with your bullying parent and everywhere you go.

JOURNAL PROMPTS

1. How would you describe the strength required to deal with your parental bully?

2. If more strength is required of you, how might you "grow" it?

3. What strengths do you bring to the table?

Chapter 27

ENLIST ALLIES

Victims of parental bullying regularly express how maintaining contact with family members who saw the situation the same way that they did was their primary healing and survival strategy (other than establishing physical distance).

For example, sisters might support one another in validating their memories ("Yes, Anna, it really was that bad!") and standing together in mutual defense and ongoing defiance of the authoritarian parent. Whether or not you are still in close contact with your bullying parent, it will reward you to identify allies and then begin the process of reaching out to those allies.

Rhonda, for example, explained: "When I try to go it alone, I can't deal with my mother. But when I'm with my sisters, the whole thing seems less tragic. I think that's why we live close to one another; that very proximity is a kind of armor against Mom's assaults. I remember when I had to go see Mom on a piece of legal business. I was so dreading it that I was making myself sick. Finally, my sisters both announced, 'We're coming with you!' They did; I survived; and their company—I would say, protection—made all the difference in the world."

What do children try to do to protect themselves in an abusive family? According to researchers writing in *Child and Adolescent*

Social Work Journal, in an article called "Adaptation and Coping in Childhood and Adolescence for those at Risk for Depression in Emerging Adulthood," the two primary methods children employed were planned evasion and an active search for support. The researchers explained:

> Respondents did not describe themselves as passive, nor in denial of the circumstances that made their lives difficult. Instead, they talked about the evasion of adversity, most often when they were quite young, as an active and planned-out strategy for protecting themselves from harm. They also stressed the importance of social support in their lives. According to their stories, help from adults and peers seemed to help decrease feelings of isolation and of being overwhelmed by their difficulties. Seeking out other people and asking for help offered an avenue to find ways of coping that the participants may not have found alone.

Find those with whom you can make alliances. Make an ally in your own family if you can. Is there someone in your extended family who gets that you are being bullied and who sees that as not okay? That someone might be a grandparent, an aunt or uncle, or a cousin— technology being what it is, it's easy to stay in touch with your ally even if he or she lives halfway around the world. That person might become a confidant, someone you can talk to so that your feelings don't get bottled up and your experiences don't go unacknowledged.

An ally is more than just a confidant. It is someone with whom you can strategically plan, and someone who may be in a position to actually intervene or help in some other way. Make a list of everyone in your family, no matter how old or young or how geographically close or distant, and star the names of your ally candidates. Then reach out to one of your starred candidates and say, "I need to tell you something. May I?" See how reaching out goes.

If that particular relationship doesn't pan out—if that family member doesn't seem interested enough or sympathetic enough—try the next starred person on your list. Give making at least one family ally a try! You might even try someone who said no to you in years past, since that person may have changed his or her mind, maybe as a result of having more contact with your bullying parent. Revisit potential allies, even if you don't hold out much hope that they will have changed their mind.

That change of mind does happen. Ralph recalled, "My uncle Rob, my father's brother, held to the idea that his brother was perfectly okay. He didn't see any of the behaviors I described and stopped just short of saying that I must be making it all up. He was sympathetic, but he simply didn't believe me. Then came a moment when they had to divide up the family estate, which was small but not insignificant. And boy, did Rob get some firsthand bullying! At first, he didn't believe it—he was seeing it with his own eyes, but he still couldn't quite accept what he was seeing. Then he had to believe it. And he apologized for not believing me—which was one of the highlights of my life."

Whether or not you can make an ally within your family, try to make allies outside of your family. You can't have too many allies! You might reach out to a teacher, a school counselor, a coach, a Sunday school teacher, or a professional like a social worker, whose job it is to protect you. It can be scary to reach out, to reveal family secrets, and to perhaps start a process that may ultimately involve social services and the criminal justice system. Of course, reaching out outside the family might cause huge disruptions and changes in your life. It's clear why you might be reluctant to reach out. But if you're being harmed, consider reaching out and looking for allies as one of your options.

If you are now an adult and currently geographically far removed from your bullying parent, you may still benefit from allies. Remember that physical separation is one thing and psychological separation is another. Allies may be able to help you maintain the psychological separation you need, talk you out of making unnecessary visits home, remind you that what happened really did happen, and in other important ways look out for your safety and support your healing. Allies are valuable: bring some into your life.

JOURNAL PROMPTS

1. Do you currently have any allies?

2. If not, is it because you're reluctant to reach out? What might help you decide to reach out?

3. What sort of help would you like an ally to provide?

Chapter 28

ACKNOWLEDGE TRAUMA

Ongoing parental bullying is the equivalent of a series of traumatic events. Have you really acknowledged all that trauma? Maybe you've tried to minimize it or forget it, and maybe you'd like to wish it away. But it happened—and it matters. If you haven't really acknowledged it yet, now is the time to do so.

Trauma creates a certain sort of shattering. What gets shattered? Sometimes it's our sense of safety. The world no longer feels safe to us. Sometimes it's our self-esteem and our self-image. We drop down many pegs in our own estimation and no longer see ourselves as competent, loveable, or worthy. Sometimes it's our basic relationship to life. One moment life was our oyster, and the next moment life felt like a cheat. Trauma is a shattering.

The other day, I was moving a wine glass from the dishwasher to the cupboard and accidentally hit the wine glass hard against the edge of the cupboard door. The glass completely cracked but didn't shatter. It held itself together by a hair. You could tell that with the slightest movement, the slightest disruption, it would shatter into many pieces. Trauma can operate like this, too. Maybe the trauma you experience doesn't shatter you, but it cracks you in such a way that you are barely holding yourself together. You are forced to tiptoe through life, holding your breath, so that you don't shatter.

What can cause such traumas? Really, almost anything. Not just rapes, car accidents, wars, and parental beatings—anything. The great existential writers understood trauma more deeply and more honestly than do contemporary mental health professionals, who limit the kinds of experiences that they are willing to consider traumatic. But there are no such limits in reality. Anything can be experienced as traumatic, if it is experienced that way. That single unkind thing your mother said, that small, restrained, violent gesture your father made, if those are experienced as traumatic, then that's exactly what they are.

Any experience that pierces our psyche, harms our self-image, makes the world feel significantly scarier, and changes our basic relationship to life—anything that shatters us or cracks us—is a traumatic experience. Maybe sometimes it's an objectively terrible experience that produces the trauma, like one of those terrifying events described in the first part of this book. But objectively trifling experiences can produce trauma, too. The only real test as to whether an experience is traumatic is if you experience it as traumatic.

In *The Stranger*, Albert Camus described how a meaningless day could be experienced as so traumatic as to lead to a pointless murder. Jean-Paul Sartre, in his classic novel *Nausea*, has the protagonist find his world shattered by the traumatic experience of *encountering a tree*; in that split second, the protagonist saw through to the nothingness behind physical reality. In *Notes from Underground*, Fyodor Dostoevsky helps us understand that when a man of lower rank is led about by the nose by a man of higher rank, *both men might be traumatized by that experience*. The great existential writers understood this.

Anything can be experienced as traumatic, including looking out of your window and no longer recognizing the world. Only you get to say what has proven traumatic to you or what may prove traumatic for you. This is a big headline, because we have been trained to believe that it is the size of the incident that determines whether or not a traumatic event has occurred. But that isn't what determines whether or not we will experience some event as traumatic. It is our inner reality that determines it, our precise idiosyncratic makeup, not the so-to-speak magnitude of the event.

For me, three months of needing a catheter was a much less traumatic experience than the superficial cut I gave myself carving a Thanksgiving turkey one Thanksgiving Thursday. I experienced that cut as other-worldly, as a shattering, and that catheter as a mere inconvenience. Yes, you're certainly more likely to be traumatized by being humiliated by your bullying parent than by cutting your finger, and more likely by being constantly scrutinized than by finding yourself bored on a Sunday afternoon. Of course. But unless we understand the extent to which a cut or a dull day can prove traumatic, we won't really understand the nature of trauma.

Maybe you learned to somehow deal with your father's intrusiveness. But there was that one time when he pushed open your door...and that time felt different. Maybe "nothing happened"—but you know in your heart that you were badly frightened and that you maybe even got cracked or shattered. Maybe in that split second, you lost your sense of trust—and still haven't regained it. "Nothing much" happened—just your door opening unexpectedly. But of course, a giant thing happened.

Let me give you the gift of permission to experience life exactly as you really experience it. What is trauma? What you have experienced as traumatic. The shattering and the cracking you've experienced are as real as that cracked wine glass barely holding itself together or the blood flowing from that Thanksgiving cut. Without knowing it, you have been trained to believe that you shouldn't be upset by "innocuous" events, by some small slight, some cross word, some mere disappointment. This way of thinking robs you of permission to honor what you actually felt: traumatized.

JOURNAL PROMPTS

1. Did you experience your parental bullying as traumatic?

2. If you haven't quite ever acknowledged the traumatic nature of that bullying, do you believe that it would serve you to do so now?

3. How might you acknowledge that trauma? By writing about it? By telling someone? By confronting someone. In some other way?

Chapter 29

LISTEN TO YOUR BODY

Trauma lives on in your personality, in your thoughts, in your feelings, and in your behaviors. But it also lives on in your body.

It lives on by harming your immune system, opening you up to opportunistic illnesses. It lives on by contributing to fatigue and by causing sleeplessness that further wears down your system. We do not clearly understand the ways in which trauma may be implicated in ailments like arthritis, irritable bowel syndrome, chronic fatigue syndrome, and countless others, but we ought to be alert to possible causal and contributory connections. Trauma is bad for your emotional well-being, but it is also bad for your health.

It therefore follows that healing trauma helps heal your body. It also helps you strengthen your resistance to ailments. As you're engaged in your healing process, you will want to listen to your body and learn from your own inner intuition whether a physical ailment is likely "purely medical" or whether it may have its roots in your experience of trauma.

Of course, it isn't at all easy to make such determinations with any accuracy. And making such a determination is made that much harder by the medical establishment's pressure on you to believe that whatever you are experiencing is best addressed with a pill. But despite that opaqueness and that pressure, trying to intuitively fathom the connection between trauma and physical health is a valuable exercise.

Even though you may not be able to get a clear understanding of what is going on in and with your body, it can still pay great dividends to simply wonder, "Might doing healing work around my traumatic experiences go a long way toward mending my body?" It goes without saying that there is a connection between our mind and our body. But the truth of the matter goes far beyond that obvious, incontrovertible connection. The burden that we carry from trauma circulates within us; and ridding ourselves of that circulating trauma is bound to improve our physical health.

How might you rid yourself of that circulating trauma?

One way is through the use of guided visualizations. It's likely that you already know about the processes called "guided visualizations," but let me spend a moment describing them. A guided visualization is a series of pictures you paint for yourself in your mind's eye with the intention of achieving some desired state or goal. That state might be calmness, or that goal might be hitting a golf ball down the middle of the fairway with accuracy. You picture what you are aiming for and, by picturing it, help make it happen.

Modern medical uses of guided visualizations started out as aids to cancer treatment. Patients were invited to picture their healthy cells defeating their cancerous cells. You can use your guided visualization in a similar way. Maybe you would like to create a guided visualization where you see the toxins of trauma leaving your body. You can do this picturing any way you like. Your idiosyncratic guided visualization might involve picturing uninvited guests leaving a party, woman warrior cells battling your toxic trauma cells, or gentle cellular cleansing involving bath oils and soft sponges.

Please take a little time and create a guided visualization of your own that feels right to you and that you can use as an aid in removing the effects of trauma from your body. And having created it, please use it. You may not have any perfect way of knowing how trauma is affecting your physical health, but you can work on healing your body even without knowing what those effects may be. One way is by adding the guided visualization you just created to your morning self-care routine.

Jennifer offered up the following observations: "I was abused by my father in all sorts of ways. That messed with my mind—that I've always understood. But until recently I didn't understand the connection between that abuse and the many, many strange physical complaints I've had. Maybe there isn't really a connection—I mean, how can I really know? But it just feels as if there is, and a kind of proof is how sick I get not only seeing my dad but even thinking about seeing my dad. I come down with real fevers—not imaginary fevers, but real fevers; I ache; I can hardly move my body. It's got to be connected, doesn't it?"

Robert offered this: "I'm an athlete—a professional athlete. I'm in top physical shape—usually. Of course, I sometimes get injured; but I don't mean that. It's this other thing, the migraines I get. My parents were always on me growing up, which helped me excel but which also exhausted me. Now, if I know that they're coming to a game, that I'm going to have to see them, I get these terrible, ferocious migraines. I'm told that they're physical, not psychological, and of course they are physical—I mean, of course, it's a body thing. But the why of it? That's got to be psychological. I dread seeing my parents, especially on game day, and that dread gives me wicked headaches."

If you are willing to spend just a few minutes every morning calmly and mindfully removing the toxins of trauma from your system via a guided visualization or in some other way, that is bound to produce health benefits. Please give this healing practice a daily try.

JOURNAL PROMPTS

1. Do you have the sense that there is a connection between your experience of parental bullying and your physical health?

2. Can you describe some of those connections, as you intuit them?

3. If you do sense that sort of connection, what does that suggest you try in order to heal your body?

Chapter 30

PRACTICE CALM SELF-AWARENESS

If you've been traumatized, it can feel better to stay unaware. "Not noticing" may have helped you deal with your traumatic experiences. As a result, "not noticing" may have become a habitual stance and a default way of being. If that has happened, then you may fail to notice triggers and be forced to deal with a sudden flood of painful emotions; you may fail to notice that you are repeating a pattern, like choosing authoritarian life partners, and find yourself in another abusive relationship; you may fail to notice how enraged you are just below the surface and lash out without knowing why; and in countless other ways you may let that habit of "not noticing" reduce your freedom and prevent you from genuinely healing.

How can you acquire this "skill of awareness"? By calmly stepping to the side and asking "Why?" rather more often than you may currently be doing. For instance, you might find yourself asking: "Why did I lash out at Bob when I really had no intention of picking a fight?" Or: "Why do I keep telling myself that I have no talent when I know that thought can't possibly serve me?" Or: "Why have I decided that life is a cheat and not worth living?" Or: "Why I am still giving power to my parents when I know that interacting with them only harms me?" Or: "Why do I refuse to give up 'friendships' with people I don't even like?" The trick is to step to the side and bravely consider what you notice.

The habit of awareness is stepping to the side, asking yourself why, staying put, weathering the anxiety that comes with asking yourself hard questions, and doing the inner work required to answer your own questions. Expect that anxiety. It makes us anxious to look at matters as difficult as our own self-sabotaging behaviors or our own limiting thoughts. Because this work will make you anxious, you also need to cultivate the habit of calmness. Cultivating those two related habits, calmness and awareness, will allow you to make the changes that you know that you want to make and that will help you heal.

Mindfulness is the word we have come to use to stand for many positive traits with names like calmness, awareness, and thoughtfulness. Mindfulness is often said in the same breath as meditation, as in "mindful meditation," but mindfulness is not necessarily connected to the formal practice of meditation. Rather, at its heart, it is a *stance* that a person *decides* to take: the stance of a person who has decided to become aware rather than to remain defensively blind.

This stance is the key to healing trauma, dealing with your bullying parents, and living your life purposes. No other tactic, strategy, method, or practice will make that much difference if you haven't committed to getting a grip on your own mind and to living mindfully. However, this is no easy task. One of the ways that we deal with trauma when it is occurring is by dissociating: that is, by *not* being aware and by internally separating ourselves from the situation.

This is a natural human safety measure, which means that it is part of our evolutionary nature to make use of a lack of awareness to protect ourselves. If denial, defensiveness, dissociation, and similar safety measures that cause us to stay unaware are built right into us, doesn't that perhaps mean that a lack of awareness is a good way to deal with trauma? No. It only means that when we are desperate and really want to get away but can't get away, our body and mind resort to such tactics because they seem like—and sometimes genuinely may be—the only options available to us. We don't have a great repertoire of better measures than fight, flight, or freeze—until we make self-awareness a habit.

Because trauma is genuinely terrible, and because we have no great way of dealing with something really terrible, we do the best that we can by becoming unaware. A lack of awareness as a response has evolutionary roots and may even be our default way of dealing with danger. But as a general rule and for the sake of better self-protection, awareness is better.

Remember that mindful awareness is not the same as hypervigilance, nor is it the same as paying attention to matters that you do not want to be thinking about. You do not need to stay aware of every stray noise, and you do not need to know anything about two world news unless you have decided that it serves you to know. Being aware is not the same as being aware of everything. In fact, the essence of mindful awareness is choosing where you will pay attention and where you won't. Mindfulness is a process of selection and filtering.

You want to pay attention where you ought to be paying attention. This stance of attentive mindfulness will help you with every aspect of your life, including recognizing the effects of trauma or preparing yourself for a visit to the family home. Calm self-awareness helps you notice that you are reacting to a family situation not as you would really like to react, but as your formed personality is pressuring you to react. It alerts you to triggering situations, to circumstances that are somehow connected to past traumatic experiences and that are likely going to flood you with powerful, terrible feelings. This bold, rather rare stance of being thoughtful and aware rather than reactive and defensive is a gift that is in your power to give yourself.

Because it may *seem* as if a lack of awareness protects you better than calm self-awareness does, you may have gotten into the habit—maybe even the lifelong habit—of distrusting awareness. That is a good question to ponder today. Do you believe in awareness, or do you actually believe that a lack of awareness is the safer bet? How would you answer that question? And what if you discover that you don't really believe in calm self-awareness all that much? Snap your fingers and change your mind. Make an instant, brilliant shift in the direction of embracing thoughtfulness.

To begin with, you may not love being so aware. It may feel odd, disquieting, and even dangerous to see that clearly. You may suddenly see that you have some huge changes to make. Keep breathing; continue to encourage yourself to stay on this new path of calm self-awareness. Sense how this path will ultimately serve you beautifully, even if right now it feels like you've precipitated an earthquake. To begin with, practicing calm self-awareness may make you feel anything but calm. But trust the process!

JOURNAL PROMPTS

1. How would you describe "self-awareness"?

2. What do you see as the difference between "agitated self-awareness" and "calm self-awareness"?

3. What might you try in order to cultivate the habit of calm self-awareness?

Chapter 31

PRACTICE SELF-CARE

Practicing self-care is no simple matter. How exactly are you supposed to effectively care for yourself while burdened by the effects of trauma, by the rigors of living, and by the sheer weight of everything? Are squeezing in a hot shower or a walk in the woods really going to do the trick? If they are lovely but hardly enough, what sort of self-care are we talking about?

First of all, what do we mean by self-care? It's likely that everyone has a different idea of what that phrase means. Lynda Monk, a colleague of mine who's been running self-care workshops for decades, shared with me the following:

In my self-care workshops, I ask participants this question: What is self-care? Here are some of the common responses to this question:

- Any action we take on our own behalf that helps us feel relaxed, joyful, and well

- An attitude: I am worthy of respect and attention

- Self-care isn't selfish (guilt-free self-care)

- Self-care is an investment in your health and well-being

- Self-care helps with work-life balance

- Self-care helps with boundary-setting and setting limits

- Self-care is essential for managing stress

- Self-care is how you fill your own cup and replenish your energy

- Self-care involves treating yourself as someone you really care about, including being kind and compassionate toward yourself

The essence of self-care is trying out things that might work to help you heal and feel well, seeing which do work, and then systematically using those that work. This is a process of experimentation and accumulation since your goal is to accumulate many helping strategies, tactics, and tools. It's unlikely that any one thing—therapy, hot showers, right thinking, or a healthy diet—will prove to be the complete answer by itself. Taken together, however, the many things you discover that do help may make a major difference.

Here's an excellent example of the experience of that accumulation of self-care tools, provided to me by Michael, a well-known French writer and visual artist:

I was sexually abused as a child at age eleven by my uncle, and I also suffered prolonged emotional, psychological, and physical abuse while growing up, in particular from my father. For example, a situation that comes to mind is of being suddenly slapped in the face while my father was struggling with getting ice cubes from a tray. The randomness of the event was typical. It created a hypervigilance in me because I could never tell when or how 'lightning' would strike.

I was identified as experiencing anxiety by a psychiatrist and given medication for it. I went to him for what I thought was depression, but it was identified instead as anxiety. I believe this was connected to the trauma, because whenever I tried to write about my experiences, this 'white noise' would start up in my mind, making it very hard to 'hear' what it was I needed to write. Medication was very useful in the beginning to deal with this. It quieted that inner noise enough so I could actually think through what it was I needed to think through. Finally, I could write.

Medication helped with the symptoms of anxiety but (unfortunately) didn't prove useful over the longer term. The effects of the medication would wear off, and I would have to slowly increase the dosage. This worried me, and I realized that medication had a limited time span. Thus, I knew that I needed to try other things as well. There have been a range of other things I've tried, and all of them have helped a bit, though none was a complete answer in itself. These included:

- Meditation (again, over a very long time, in excess of ten years) helped a bit.
- Cognitive-behavioral therapy helped a bit.
- Men's groups and workshops on sexual abuse have helped.
- Physical exercise like intensive yoga or working with heavy weights has helped a bit.

- Engaging in long-term talk therapy has helped.

- Writing—both creative and journaling—has helped.

- Traditional Chinese medicine and qigong have helped.

Lots of things have helped a bit, but more importantly, all of them together have helped a lot. I am finding long-term benefits in writing, especially intensive, serious, and questioning journaling that does much more than simply describe my day. This has helped me rediscover and nurture my voice, and I feel more connected to myself because of this.

Michael's efforts may well mirror yours. I am calling self-care a tool or skill because we can get better at it. We can get better at self-care by mindfully paying attention to what works and what doesn't work to help us maintain our equilibrium and our emotional well-being. No single tactic may prove to be enough; but a robust menu of them may amount to enough help to transform your present-day experience.

We want to make sure not to forget about existential self-care: that is, self-care with regard to our life purpose choices and our meaning-making efforts. We would love life to come with slogan-sized affirmations and admonitions. But is it really so easy to know how to maneuver when old jobs vanish and new jobs require our complete retraining? Is it really so easy to know what to do if our son is an alcoholic or if our parents are growing more confused daily? Is any of this easy to deal with, either practically or existentially?

Are slogans like "Just do it!" or "Everything is for the best!" really up to such challenges? They aren't. Life is exactly as complex as it is. To hunger for a simplicity that doesn't exist is to breed sadness. Existential self-care includes reckoning with these realities and making strong life purpose choices even while perplexed and uncertain. A hot shower does the kind of work it does; identifying your life purposes and then living them does very different yet important work.

It is crucial that you know what matters to you—even if that keeps shifting. If you are always merely surviving, that is exactly how life will feel to you. It will feel like a burdensome thing and a source of sadness. But if you have a sense of what matters to you, what you are trying to accomplish, what you are trying to uphold, what you want your life to feel like and represent—if you have a sense of what matters to you, you can hold sadness at bay. Identifying what matters to you and then living in the light of those choices is existential self-care at its best.

I get to decide what will make me feel righteous and happy, and you get to decide what will make you feel righteous and happy. A person can move all the way from wondering what the universe wants of them, to announcing that they can make life mean exactly what they intend it to mean. The instant that you realize that meaning is neither provided, as traditional belief systems teach, nor absent, as nihilists feel, a new world of potential opens up for you. You have aimed yourself in a brilliant direction: the path of your own creation.

Existential self-help consists of grounding yourself in a pair of realities, that life is exactly as it is and that you are obliged to keep your head up and make yourself proud. Most people make the mistake of supposing that if they don't look life squarely in the eye, they can avoid noticing what's making them unhappy. Instead of their dodge proving successful, they simply increase their unhappiness.

By accepting the realities of life, by announcing that you intend to direct life as best you can, and by asserting that what matters to you is what you decide matters to you, you stand up straight—and that gesture of getting to your feet is the epitome of self-care.

JOURNAL PROMPTS

1. What does the phrase "self-care" mean to you?

2. What do you know to do to provide yourself with self-care?

3. What new self-care strategies might you like to try?

Chapter 32

STAY ALERT
FOR TRIGGERS

In the language of the twelve-step recovery movement, a trigger is an internal or external cue that is likely to cause a person in recovery to relapse and resume his or her addictive behavior.

A trigger might be the appearance of a certain feeling, like feeling overwhelmed. It might be seeing someone in a film or a television show who is having an experience like one you've had. It might be encountering a certain smell, like an aftershave lotion, or a certain sound, like a door slamming. You will want to identify your triggers, anticipate them, be on the watch for them, and create a plan of action to deal with them.

Marvin put it this way: "I used street drugs to deal with my feelings of worthlessness, feelings that were the product of growing up with a really mean, shaming dad. Once I entered recovery, I had to figure out what my triggers were. One sneaky one was seeing some random man wearing a knit cap like the one my father used to wear. That was always a trigger; and I knew exactly what to do: Get myself to a meeting."

A trigger is anything that causes you to re-experience trauma or that produces one or another of the toxic effects of trauma, like despair or high anxiety. The better you can identify your triggers, anticipate them, and be on the lookout for them, the better you can do one of two things: Avoid them, if they can be avoided; or prepare to deal with them as effectively as possible, if they can't be avoided.

A trigger can be anything—a person, a smell, a sight, a sound, a place, a thought, a feeling, or even just a certain look to the sky. Knowing how you're triggered is great learning. It is also painful learning, since you are forced to learn about your triggers through experience, which means that you are bound to have painful experiences. However, once you have learned about them through experience, you will then know what triggers you.

Unfortunately, this will prove to be imperfect and incomplete knowledge, because something new and unexpected may trigger you. A song or sight that never affected you before may suddenly bring back memories or flood you with feelings. This sort of learning can last a lifetime. Still, with experience, you will acquire an understanding of at least your primary triggers. This knowledge will give you the chance to avoid the ones that can be avoided and better deal with the ones that can't be avoided or that pop up to surprise you.

See if you can put together a list of your triggers. The list can be as short or as long as you like. Once you've created your list, your next step would be to take each trigger in turn and ask yourself, "How can I avoid this trigger?" or "How can I best deal with this trigger, if I can't avoid it?" Here's an example of what I mean.

Say that there is a bridge just outside of town that triggers suicidal thoughts in you. If there are many ways to go where you need to go each day, you would create the clear intention to avoid that bridge and take some other route. You would avoid that trigger.

On the other hand, you could be stuck needing to take that one particular bridge because it is the only way out of town, and unless and until you move somewhere else, you will need to know what you intend to do to deal with the fact that you must face that triggering bridge twice a day, when you leave for work and when you come home from work. What will you do? Play loud music to drown out sensations during the crossing? Listen to a calming meditation? The one thing you can't do is close your eyes—that won't work!

I think you can see how a person might become paralyzed in life through efforts to avoid his or her triggers. Say that you didn't quite realize the extent to which that bridge was a trigger, but you knew somewhere inside of you that you wanted to avoid it at all costs. And let's say that you were obliged to cross it to get where you needed to go each day because there was no other route out of town. You might well make the decision, just out of conscious awareness, never to go anywhere near that bridge—which would be tantamount to deciding that you could never leave town.

In order to avoid that bridge, you might even become housebound— without having a conscious understanding of what was going on. Take a look at your own circumstances, think it through, and notice if anything like that is going on in your life. Are you avoiding a painful trigger—a particular family gathering, a particular sibling conversation—without quite knowing that you are engaged in that avoidance? If some defensiveness of that sort is going on, it would be good to know. You might still want to avoid that gathering or that conversation, but now you would at least have a clearer understanding of why.

Encountering a trigger has effects. Unconsciously avoiding a trigger also has effects. If the bullying is still occurring, there will likely be triggers all around you: triggers like every car door slamming outside, signaling to you that your abusive parent may be returning home. If the bullying happened in the past, you may experience fewer triggers nowadays—but the ones you do experience may still prove powerfully triggering. This is a subject that will repay your effort spent in exploring.

JOURNAL PROMPTS

1. Describe the idea of "triggers" in your own words.

2. Can you create a list of triggers? Does that seem like something that would prove valuable to do?

3. For each trigger on your list, try to figure out if the trigger can or can't be avoided. If it can be avoided, how will you avoid it? If it can't be avoided, how will you deal with it when you are forced to encounter it?

Chapter 33

CREATE A SUPPORT SYSTEM

Fundamentally, we must go it alone in life. But we can also make the choice to go through life together: to love, to have friends, to seek out peer support, to not isolate or withdraw. Going it alone is an existential given. Being in it with others is a choice.

Maria explained, "I have to be able to handle things on my own, because, growing up, I lost so much power and so much self-confidence that my goal for myself is to be powerful and self-confident. However, that doesn't mean that I have to handle every single thing alone. So, I've created a kind of informal support team. I don't turn to them first thing—first, I want to trust my own resources. But I'm not stubborn and I do turn to them just as soon as I understand that I could use some help!"

The experience of trauma can make it that much harder to seek out support. Trauma can feel shaming and humiliating, causing us to withdraw and hide. Trauma can make the world feel that much scarier, causing us to mistrust others. Many of the consequences of trauma naturally push us in the direction of isolation and away from relationships.

Still, we can strive to override that push toward isolation and make the choice to connect. We can join a support group and feel supported. We can make a friend and experience friendship with them. Best of all, if we are lucky and if we make the effort, we can share our life with one intimate other who is on our side, and making life feel much less alienating and burdensome.

I hope that you will want to make that choice, because life feels warmer, more meaningful, and altogether better when we connect with others, especially with one intimate other. What helps with establishing that connection? Bringing the same stance of mindful awareness and the same skills we've discussed previously to your efforts to create a supportive relationship can make a crucial difference.

Given that half of first marriages and almost three-quarters of second and third marriages end in divorce, it's clear that the road is rocky for virtually everyone.

Skills are required! If you opt for relating and want to create a strong relationship with one intimate other, here are a dozen keys to making that relationship work:

1. Be friendly. Nothing is more crucial to the viability of an intimate relationship than that the partners are friendly toward one another; and friendship, like love, requires its own sort of care and attention.

2. Care for each other's solitude. It must be all right and more than all right for each partner to spend significant amounts of time pursuing his or her own activities and communing with his or her own inner life.

3. Provide emotional security. When the people in a relationship are doing this, each partner is not only aware of the other's feelings but takes them into account and actively works to help his or her partner feel good rather than bad.

4. Meet meaning needs. Each partner needs to understand that meaning comes and goes and that meaning crises will inevitably arise and will require both partners' attention; and they need to bear in mind that identifying shared values and principles is a key to meaning maintenance.

5. Maintain passion. Partners can make (and keep) a commitment not to let themselves become too busy for love and intimacy, too tired for love and intimacy, or too disinterested in love and intimacy.

6. Gently exchange truths. When there is something that must be said, it should be said carefully and compassionately—as well as clearly and directly.

7. Accept difficulty. While partners will naturally expect a lot from themselves and from their partner, they will also recognize and accept that failures of nerve, bleak moods, and pratfalls do happen.

8. Minimize your own unwanted qualities. Each partner will bravely look in the mirror, take a fearless personal inventory, identify, and then work to change those aspects of their formed personality that harm the relationship.

9. Manage your own journey. Each partner has the job of taking responsibility for his or her own life, for setting goals and planning, for making choices and taking action, and for

proceeding as a responsible adult—of course in consultation with your partner.

10. Treat each other fairly. Fairness in everything—in the honoring of agreements, the equitable distribution of resources and opportunities, the respect shown in word and deed: That's the glue that holds a healthy relationship together.

11. Create at least occasional happiness. Partners will actually ask questions of each other like, "What would make us happy?" and, "What would make you happy?"

12. Create a truly supportive relationship. Even if two people find it easy to relate, they will still have to invest time and pay attention to this thing they have created together: a real relationship.

The support of even just one other person can make a tremendous difference. Whether or not you are in an intimate relationship and have the support of an intimate other, you can organize support in a multitude of other ways: through friendships, through paid counseling or coaching, by joining a twelve-step group or a support group, by rallying family allies, by joining clubs and organizations whose mission may not be to provide support but whose members are informally supportive of one another, by forming a small support group or circle of friends who meet regularly, through church opportunities, via affinity groups or mastermind groups, and in countless other ways.

Carol explained: "I'm not currently in a relationship. I've found relationships hard, and I'm taking a break from getting involved with anyone too intensely right now. I've been burned and need a break.

But I'm still coping with tremendous family drama, and I haven't wanted to deal with that all by myself. So, I joined a support group run by my HMO—I had no idea they provided such a service, but I happened upon a flyer in the hospital lobby and decided to give them a try. And it's made a pretty significant difference. They use certain twelve-step principles like not permitting crosstalk, and the woman who runs it is both firm and kind. It is helping a lot."

Jack shared: "I am not a joiner. I loved sports, but I never played team sports because I didn't want to be bullied by a coach. I'd had enough bullying at home. So, I swam, played tennis, and ran marathons—individual things. At work, too, which is a high-pressure environment, I didn't go out with the guys for long lunches or pal around after work. Working remotely suited me just fine! But I did begin to realize that I was just too isolated and too unsupported. I needed someone to talk to. And it turned out to be the last person in the world I thought it would be—my rabbi. He's young, he doesn't bully, he has a twinkle in his eye, and he's got that right mix of listening and suggesting. We don't meet often, but I know he's there, like a sponsor in AA; and when I need to talk, I get in touch with him right away."

Parental bullying and trauma can harm our ability to relate. Since love, warmth, and human support are excellent things, we don't want to give up on relating just because we've been harmed by trauma. Rather, we can choose ways to mindfully relate and actively work on creating the healthy relationships we crave. This is an important part of the recovery process and of mindful living.

JOURNAL PROMPTS

1. Do you see creating a support system as something important to do? If not, what seems to be getting in the way of considering that possibility?

2. Do you currently have a support system in place? Can you describe it?

3. If you don't have a support system in place, do you have at least one person you can talk to? If not, might you want to try and cultivate at least one such supportive relationship?

Chapter 34

RELEASE GUILT AND SHAME

Survivors of parental bullying typically experience guilt. Some felt guilty about not protecting their younger siblings from the family dictator. Some feel guilty about having failed themselves or not having lived up to their potential. Some feel guilty about physically or emotionally separating from their authoritarian parent. Some feel guilty about having contributed to their own physical problems by not doing a better job of healing their psychological wounds.

Maryanne explained, "I kept hearing myself say, 'I should go see dad, after all, he is my dad.' But it scared me to see him, and I knew better than to go see him. So, I never went—and I felt tremendously guilty about that. Then I began working with a cognitive-behavioral therapist. I really didn't believe that CBT could possibly go deep enough; I had the prejudice that it was a shallow kind of thing. But as I got into the habit of actually substituting a thought I wanted to think for the constant 'I should see dad,' I began to stop thinking that thought; and the guilt kind of melted away. I'm guessing that not everybody gets that lucky, but I did!"

Jeffrey shared: "It's hard to put words to my sense of guilt. Something happened when I was a boy that was 'close' to sexual abuse but maybe didn't rise to the level of 'real' sexual abuse? But I've felt guilty ever since. Guilty about what? Letting it happen? But I was just a boy. Not mentioning it to anyone? But I was just a boy. I'm amazed that something so less terrible than what other kids have experienced should still matter to me so much. I simply can't get it out of my mind. Maybe I'm feeling guilty about feeling guilty! It's maddening not to be able to shake this off—and it's getting worse. It's getting to the point where I feel like hiding myself away in our basement and not dealing with anyone or anything."

Many victims experience guilt. Many experience shame as well. The original shaming doesn't have to have been a "big deal" for it to have had a profound effect. Irina recalled the following "small" incident:

> When I was around five, I had great fun at an art class in school. I brought my drawing home, and my mother showed it around to the other adults who happened to be there that day—my uncles and aunts—and exclaimed with that harsh laugh of hers, "Well, that was a waste of good paper!" She crumbled it up and threw it away and everybody laughed.
>
> I think that this incident had a profound impact on me. To this day, I like making art but have great difficulties showing my work to anyone. I am content to create, but I am not brave enough to readily invite criticism or rejection. But I do believe that I can change the way that the incident negatively affects me by remembering that even though I don't feel comfortable showing my work publicly, I have done so on several occasions. As an art student in art and photo classes, I took part in several exhibitions. So, I have been brave before!
>
> I can put that childhood experience behind me by remembering that I *can* be brave enough to show my work when required because I *have* already done so before. Remembering what I was capable of before will hopefully help me build my creative

confidence now that I have started making art again after a long hiatus. But it's really quite terrible that such a "small" moment of shaming has harmed me so much—terrible and incredible.

For many adults, a place of ongoing shame is how they look. Here is how Gina helped herself deal with and heal from that particular shame:

Since it's impossible to get rid of every mirror in the world, I decided that I had to "deal with mirrors." First, I tried to think up an affirmation or a "right thought" that would serve me, something to think whenever I accidentally or intentionally saw myself in a mirror. After many tries, I came up with a really helpful one: "I will love myself when I see myself."

That process started me on a path of genuine self-forgiveness. Now I am committed to forgive myself for all the ways in which I have not accepted the body I actually have, rather than some other body I imagine I could have. And I also now forgive myself for all the ways in which I have not accepted the career and life I actually have, rather than some other career and life I imagine I could have had!

As I did this "mirror work," I began to remember when looking in the mirror was in fact a magical experience. I had been suffering with ankle pain for a year and tried out the following mirror treatment. I positioned myself in a way so that I saw the reflection of the good leg in the mirror while the injured leg was hidden from view. Moving the healthy leg and attempting to move the other at the same time, the brain only saw two healthy limbs moving perfectly together. This played a huge role in my recovery.

When I look in the mirror now, I see that my stomach is bigger than I would like. I see the wrinkles, the thinning hair. Behind all of that, I see the vitality that is me. I see the free spirit that I am, and I love her, I love myself. I see others who are my age (seventy-one), and they seem worn down and defeated. I am grateful that is not true for me, much of the time. I accept the way I am, the "who" of me. I remind myself that I am doing what I need to do to be healthy, to be at the weight I want to be, and to be stronger, and I am proud of that.

It would be lovely if you could just snap your fingers and be done with guilt and shame. Maybe such miracles are possible—no harm in trying! Snap your fingers and exclaim, "Done with that!" But if snapping your fingers doesn't quite do the trick, you may need to embark on a journey of self-inquiry and healing in order to rid yourself of these twin malignancies. It's likely that recovering from parental bullying will require that exact work.

JOURNAL PROMPTS

1. What do you see as the difference between "guilt" and "shame"?

2. Are you carrying around unnecessary guilt associated with your bullying parent or some other family member? What might help you dissipate that guilt?

3. Are you carrying around painful shame connected to your childhood experiences? Can you picture a ceremony or ritual that might help you release that shame?

Chapter 35

SPEAK UP

"Speaking up" means two very different things. It can mean telling the bully in your life what's on your mind. But it can also mean telling *yourself* what's on your mind. Trauma silences us in both ways, so that we find it hard to tell others what we need to say and just as hard, if not harder, to reveal our truth to ourselves.

Trauma is a great silencer. If speaking up was beaten out of you as a child, how likely are you to want to speak up now? If you were shamed into invisibility, how visible would you want to be now? If your opinions were ridiculed, if you were punished for having your own thoughts, if everything in your family and your culture screamed "This way only!" how quiet are you likely to have become?

Traumatic events of all sorts can silence us. Soldiers typically do not like to talk about what they saw in wartime or what they did in wartime. This silence can generalize into a morose, close-mouthed way of being where saying little or even nothing becomes the normal way. Whether the trauma was family bullying, wartime experiences, a mugging, a serious car crash, or something else, one of the results is likely a descent into silence.

Now is a day to begin to regain your voice. Nothing may feel riskier. But speaking may prove invaluable. Speaking about the trauma, say in a support group, with a peer counselor or a therapist, or to the bully in question, may serve you brilliantly. That "speaking out loud" may make all the difference in the world. But first comes speaking your truth to yourself. A first step may be speaking the words in an empty room.

Just saying them out loud may prove empowering. Once you've said them out loud, you can begin to hear how they really sound. Did they sound much less dangerous than you supposed they would? Even almost harmless? If so, that knowledge may help you feel safer and make it more likely that you will say those words "for real" out in the world and to the person in question.

Or you might use the "redesign your mind" technique we discussed earlier. Wouldn't it be wise to install a dedicated speaker's corner in the room that is your mind? Historically, the most famous speaker's corner was the northeast corner of Hyde Park in London. But there are other speaker's corners, both in England and around the world. There are speaker's corners in Indonesia, the Netherlands, Italy, Canada, Australia, Singapore, Thailand, and elsewhere. They provide a designated "safe place" for a person to speak his or her mind. In the speaker's corner that you create in the room that is your mind, *all* speech is permitted.

Self-censorship is a huge issue for all human beings. This truth helps explain why public speaking is the world's number one phobia. Most people are made profoundly anxious by having to speak in public and reveal something about themselves. Even if their talk has nothing to do with them personally—even if they are presenting sales statistics—they are still revealing how good or how poor a job they are doing at organizing their thoughts, sounding cogent and coherent, and so on. Their presentation may be about sales statistics, but *they* are on full display. That's why it can feel so scary.

How will you design your speaker's corner, and where will you put it? Will it be an old-fashioned soapbox with a megaphone, a podium with a microphone, or a spotlighted stage and a hand mic? Will you put it in a corner of the room that is your mind or in some more prominent spot? Give these details some thought right now. Situate and design your speaker's corner, then try it out. Visualize yourself standing there, speaking your truth. Picture yourself eloquent, forthright, and powerful. What do you hear yourself saying?

After that experiment may come speaking in the world. Will you finally tell your bullying parent what you've always wanted and needed to say? The prospect of that will almost certainly feel scary, if not downright terrifying. You may need to enlist your allies and your support network, you may need to rehearse what you intend to say, or you may need to revisit and maybe update your tactics for dealing with triggers and repeat trauma. It's unlikely that you're going to find this easy. But if it's valuable to speak up, and maybe more than valuable, perhaps even essential, then find the courage and speak.

Here's a small example from my coaching practice. A painter came to see me in my capacity as a creativity coach. She explained that her husband, who had recently retired, kept visiting her in her studio space to chat about inconsequential matters. I asked her to craft a sentence of seven words or fewer that communicated what she wanted to say to him about the preciousness of her painting time and space.

I knew that she had a history of family bullying. Both her mother and her father were tyrants. It thus came as no surprise to me that her first efforts were long and apologetic. Finally, after many, many tries, she arrived at: "I can't chat while I'm working."

I smiled. "Can you say that to him?" I asked.

"Yes," she replied. "Maybe. I think so."

"Imagine that you have said it. How does that feel?"

"Very, very scary."

Next, we role-played a situation she was having with the fellow who did some printing work for her. He was the only person in her area equipped to do this printing work, and she liked both the work he did and his prices. But he was always inappropriate with her, saying things like, "You know, I have feelings for you," and, "Most husbands don't understand their artist wives."

"What do you want to say to him?" I asked.

Having just practiced, she was now quicker to respond.

"I need you to stop that," she said. "I am coming here to have prints made, period." She laughed. "That's two sentences, and one's a little long. But that's the idea, right?"

"That's exactly the idea," I agreed.

First, speak up to yourself. Then decide if you want to speak up in the world, to the bully in question, to some other family member, or to someone else in your life. If you decide that you ought to speak up, rehearse what you intend to say, ready yourself, and speak. This is important work; and if you manage to pull it off, give yourself a huge pat on the back.

JOURNAL PROMPTS

1. Do you feel that you are able to tell your truth to yourself? Do you have work to do in that regard?

2. Is there something that you need to say to your bullying parent? Is it time to craft that message, rehearse it, and deliver it?

3. Try visualizing a speaker's corner in the room that is your mind. What does it look like?

Chapter 36

JOURNAL PROMPTS

Chapter 36

HONOR YOUR FREEDOM

We are both free and limited in our freedom. Victims of parental bullying tend to see the glass as half empty and view themselves as less free than they actually are. Of course, there is a lot about life that we can't control. But we can do a better job of taking charge of our own thoughts, attitudes, and actions than we typically do. To do that, we need to believe and honor that we have that kind of freedom and enough of that freedom.

That amount of freedom shifts and changes. Sometimes we are freer, sometimes less free. At a given point in our life, we may be at our least free, say for instance if we have succumbed to an addiction and have organized our life around the pull of some substance. At a different point in our life, we may be at our most free, say twenty years into sobriety, living a life of calmness, awareness, and purposefulness. Our amount of freedom can shift dramatically—and it is healing and helpful to remember that such possibilities exist. You can likely feel freer and be freer than you are now, as you do the work I've been describing.

If we give ourselves the chance, we can do a beautiful, intuitive job of feeling where we are free and where we are unfree. Ponder that question. Are you free to not visit your bullying parent as often as you currently do? Are you free to stay away *and* not feel guilty about not visiting? Are you free to speak your mind or has the cat got your tongue? Are you free to strike out in new directions and seize new meaning opportunities? Where are you shackled? Can you visualize those shackles falling away?

Imagine that personality is made up of three parts: our original personality (the endowments, proclivities, and temperament with which we come into the world); our formed personality (the way we accrete over time into our "hardened" self); and our available personality (our remaining freedom to practice awareness, make strong choices, and heal, change, and grow). Get that model in mind—original personality, formed personality, and available personality.

Now, think of some challenge that you're currently facing: Let's say despair. Part of your despair may connect to your original personality, perhaps for example to your inborn sensitivity to ideas like justice, equality, and fairness or to your stubborn individuality that the world keeps wanting to contain and thwart. Part of your despair may connect to the way that the consequences of trauma are playing themselves out in your formed personality. In this scenario, your despair is double caused, caused in part by your particular human nature and in part by your particular experiences.

In whatever ways that your despair may have been caused, you still retain some available personality—some measure of freedom to look at your despair, think about it, and try to heal and recover from it. You have *some freedom left*. It may not be a tremendous amount, but however much it is, it is real and ought not to be ignored or dismissed out of hand. This central tenet of existential thought, that we are essentially free even if we are also bound up in the chains of existence, reality, and our personality, is one of the more profound ideas of the last few hundred years. We are not completely free, but we are free *to some extent*—and that matters.

One of your healing tasks is to honor your freedom, however large or small that "amount" of freedom may be. It is not to be scorned; it is not to be dismissed as worthless; it is not to be deemed insufficient. It is to be honored and appreciated. Honor your freedom in some real way by doing something that requires it. What might that be? Giving someone a piece of your mind? Daring to spend a whole day not worrying? Celebrate and honor the extent to which you are free by doing some free thing—or just by feeling that freedom.

You might try visualizing your freedom expanding and growing. Feel yourself breaking chains and growing freer. Even if you just increase it a small amount, it counts and that matters. And if you can't grow it in this split second, if it feels too bound in chains to expand at all, still appreciate the amount that you have, even if your mind is pestering you with, "That is far too little freedom!" Appreciate the ways in which you are free, even if you wish you were more so.

Ponder the following question: "How can I grow my freedom?" Be with that question today. If you arrive at some specific answers, excellent! If no answer comes to you, still celebrate the fact that you are asking such a powerful, important, and provocative question. In case you find yourself saying to yourself, "Wow, I had no idea I was so unfree," try not to sink into a negative space. Replace that thought with, "I am going to grow my freedom." Hold that belief and that intention. Moment by moment, see if you can grow a little freer.

Remember that "freedom" and "acting out" are not the same things. Mia explained:

> My whole family was authoritarian and extremely negative. Those experiences caused me to feel a lot of negative emotions, including anxiety, stress, and anger. The first thing that I can recall about my authoritarian family is how much they made me hate them. The number one personal consequence for me due to that is resistance to authority. I have a deep inability to accept the authority of my mother and a deep-rooted hatred for how my parents raised me. I always had a desire to leave home; freedom and privacy were everything.
>
> At the same time, I was scared of losing control or being alone. There was lots of sadness and anger; hating life. I loved being a rebel or just acting out in unconventional ways and shocking everyone with controversial opinions. I've always hated being told I am not "normal," or that I'm "weird," or that something about me is "not good enough," because I know that everything is subjective and that terms like "normal" and "weird" are social constructs that are just used by those in power to keep people in line. They are there to ensure that everyone conforms to certain standards. To repeat the headlines: I'm full of hate, and I have this (not always very productive) need to rebel and act out.

Grow freer—and use your freedom wisely. You are "technically" free to drive at a hundred miles an hour after drinking a pint of vodka, but is that the wisest way to honor your freedom? You are "technically" free to marry that self-destructive, mean-spirited fellow you've "fallen in love" with after knowing him for three days—but is that you being free, or is that you making the same mistake you've made before? Be as wild as you like, but be wise. Using your freedom is not the same as honoring your freedom. Give that distinction some thought.

JOURNAL PROMPTS

1. Describe in your own words how free or unfree you are.

2. What might help you increase your freedom?

3. What might it look like to do a better job of honoring your freedom?

Chapter 37

IDENTIFY YOUR LIFE PURPOSES

A great deal of healing occurs when we live our life purposes. If we are living without purpose or if we are lost in the desert, seeking our purpose, we are much more vulnerable to the effects of trauma. If, on the other hand, we have identified our life purposes and found the way and the wherewithal to live them on a daily basis, that passionate pursuit will help us maintain meaning, forestall regrets and disappointments, handle setbacks, and live a grounded, centered life.

There is no substitute for actively living our life purposes and no better way to heal. The first step is to identify what's important to you. What are your life purposes? Maybe among them are the desire to live ethically and authentically. Maybe you see activism, being of service, intimate relationships, manifesting your creative nature, having a career, your physical and emotional health, and healing from trauma as all important to you. These, then, are your life purpose choices: your decisions about what matters to you. You get to decide; and you are obliged to decide, because until you decide, you are in effect living without purpose.

What if nothing feels that important? That is a horrible existential crisis—which millions are experiencing and must somehow endure. The main feeling that accompanies such a crisis is despair, and the main activity that accompanies such a crisis is going through the motions. In despair, you do the next thing on your to-do list, and then the next thing, somehow managing to get to the end of the day. This is not the way you want to live. You must do the following: You must proclaim that something is important.

This sounds like, "I am picking my life purposes!" Whether or not your choices feel genuinely important, you are proclaiming that they are important. Yes, this is a kind of "game." But it is a game on the side of life. This is you deciding to matter. This is you making your choices and honoring them by living them. Yes, you are clear-eyed enough to see through to the void. Yes, it may be a little on the absurd side to dub this or that as a life purpose when it is only you saying that it is. Yes, you may not be at all certain that you feel much passion for your own choices, not when you have doubts about the meaningfulness of anything and suspicions that nothing is much more important than anything else. All that notwithstanding, this is the way to live: to announce your life purpose choices and to live them.

Most people never consciously decide what's important to them. Indoctrinated in a way of thinking that makes "purpose" seem extrinsic, as if it is something out there—the proverbial "purpose of life"—they aren't helped to understand that life purpose choosing is an activity that they must engage in, a subjective reckoning about what's important and about how they intend to make themselves proud in life.

When they at last understand that they must stand up and get behind their own choices, then each day has a chance to feel meaningful. If you wake up today with the certain knowledge that you understand your own life purpose choices, and if—today—you make the effort to live some of those choices, you're likely to have a day that feels both meaningful and healing.

How does this process of identifying and living your life purposes work? Jill explained:

> The Catholicism of my childhood never worked for me, though I loved the rituals. I just didn't believe in the infallibility of the Pope or in God. That's a lot not to believe and still stay in the fold! So, I began my "spiritual journey," which has included so many paths and attempts that it would exhaust me to write them all down. This Buddhism, that Buddhism, Kabbalah, Sufiism, a thousand things with no names—alchemy, witchcraft, shamanism, vibration retreats in the Andes—that's more than enough. I have been to India and back, so to speak.
>
> Then I encountered the "simple" idea of making the switch from imagining that life had a purpose to the idea that I get to choose what's important. I can't tell you what that switch has meant to me. Now I honor my choices, which include everything from simply being present, to making fruit pies, to spending quality time with my nieces. I am done with spiritual quests that take me nowhere. I am exactly where I ought to be, where I need to be, and where I want to be.

Tom shared:

> When I encountered the idea of "identifying my life purpose choices," I got excited. That seemed like exactly what I needed to do. But almost immediately I found the going rough. What *was* important to me? I could name things, but they didn't

feel like they were meeting some unspoken "criteria" of what is important. They were only "sort of important." I got very stuck there, very confused, and a little resentful. So, I put the whole thing aside.

Then I had a dream. I was holding a child's hand crossing the street at a crosswalk. Cars had stopped to let us cross, but they were angry at having been forced to stop. They were revving their engines and threatening us. And I had such a feeling come over me, a feeling that I had to protect this child—I can't really describe it. But the dream motivated me to try again with the "life purposes" thing. This time I had a completely different experience. I put down things without reference to any mysterious "criteria"—I simply let my heart decide. And I came up with a very interesting, very peculiar, and very surprising list. I'd taken a step in the right direction and suddenly understood what "life purpose choosing" meant.

Parental bullies frequently invoke rules, ones which they themselves rarely follow and which they can change at the drop of a hat to confuse you and make you "wrong." Because of this, victims of parental bullying can have a hard time moving past the idea that the universe, too, is a rule-bound place where someone, somewhere—a god, a celebrity guru—is in charge of purpose and knows the secret to purpose. They are likely to be held hostage to the idea that life has a purpose, as if they were born indentured. Getting free of that idea and making the shift to the truer, liberating idea that we can choose what matters to us can be game-changing and lifesaving.

JOURNAL PROMPTS

1. Describe in your own words the shift from the idea that there is "a purpose to life" to the idea that life can have multiple purposes, ones that you identify and select.

2. What do you see as your current "life purposes"? What is important to you?

3. What prevents you from living your life purposes? Can you identify what may be getting in the way?

Chapter 38

LIVE YOUR
LIFE PURPOSES

It's one thing—a wonderful thing—to identify your life purposes. Knowing what's important to you, and what isn't important to you is empowering and motivating and helps you reduce your confusion, your ambient anxiety, and your despair. Engaging in the process of announcing, "This is one of my life purposes," and "This is one of my life purposes," and continuing that process until you've created a robust list or menu of life purposes is a beautiful thing.

Then you have to live those life purposes.

That isn't easy. It isn't easy to translate an abstract life purpose like being creative, being of service, becoming calmer, or becoming a better life partner into concrete actions. Even if you can name the concrete actions that go with your life purposes, it isn't easy to get them onto your daily to-do list when so much else is going on in life. Let's translate how you might accomplish that high-bar goal of actually getting to your life purposes in a daily way, broken down into a set of steps.

1. **Decide to Matter**

   The universe is not built to care about you. You must care about you. You must announce that you are opting to matter. You must announce that you are making the startling, eye-opening decision to take responsibility for your thoughts and your actions and live life instrumentally.

2. **Accept That You Must Make Meaning**

   You finally let go of the demoralizing wish that meaning would just rain down on you in a shower and accept that the only meaning that exists is the meaning that you make. You announce once and for all that you are the final arbiter of meaning in your own life. To honor this decision, you begin making meaningful investments of your effort and seizing meaningful opportunities.

3. **Identify Your Life Purposes**

   If you are going to actively make meaning in accordance with your life purposes, you had better know what your life purposes are. You need to articulate them and make sure that you really believe in them. If you aren't quite sure that you do believe in a given life purpose, you assert that you are going to act "as if" you do believe in it and stand behind it with conviction.

4. **Articulate a Life Purpose Statement**

   You list your life purposes, you perhaps rank your life purposes in order, and then you see if there is some simple statement that captures the essence of your multiple life purposes, a phrase that's easy to remember and handy to use, a phrase like, "Do the next right thing," as an example.

5. **Set and Hold the Intention to Live Your Life Purposes**

You need to keep your intentions firmly in mind. You must be able to remember your life purposes even when you're tired, bothered, distracted, upset, or otherwise not in your best frame of mind. When life resumes its habitual busyness, you must still be able to firmly hold your intentions and manifest them.

6. **Passionately Act to Fulfill Your Life Purposes**

Make some meaning in accordance with your life purposes every day. Maybe eight hours of your day are robbed from you by activities that do not align with your life purposes but which you must attend to for all the usual reasons. But some hours remain—and you must use those. Maybe you will be able to actively live your life purposes for only two or three or four hours a day—but that's likely far more than you currently accomplish. Do what you can—and honor your efforts.

7. **Institute a Morning Check-In and a Daily Routine**

Our life purpose choices—whether about dieting, writing our novel, being of service, or standing up for some cause—often get submerged under the pressures and hubbub of life. We guard against this reality by orienting ourselves first thing every day in the direction of our life purposes and by instituting a daily routine that includes our life purpose choices.

8. **Navigate the World and the Facts of Existence**

The world is not built to accommodate you. Your favorite bakery may close, or war may break out—from the smallest to the largest, the facts of existence are exactly what they are. They include pain and pleasure, loyalty and betrayal, life and death. All this you must navigate. Be brave, be mature, and be real.

9. **Create Yourself in Your Own Best Image**

You have within you undeniable strengths, as well as every manner of shadow. If you live in those shadows, you will never quite respect yourself. Do better by manifesting your strengths and by becoming the person you know you want to become. Surrender to the truth that you would prefer to be your best self.

10. **Live Your Life Purposes**

Don't idly chat about purpose, brood about purpose, endlessly look for purpose, complain about purpose, buy another book about purpose, or take a workshop on purpose: Make your life purpose choices, and live in the light of them.

Robin shared:

> I found this new language about life purposes easy to understand and completely congruent with my belief system. But my life was so crazy that I just couldn't get around to making any real use of these ideas. I got sick; I found myself caring for my aging father (whom I can't

stand); I was laid off from work... Live my life purposes? I could barely put one foot in front of the other. I still loved the idea of creating that "menu" of life purposes and living them in some powerful—or at least regular—way, but actually doing that was simply beyond me.

Then it struck me that making such a list wouldn't really take much time and might even be fun to try. I wouldn't need to treat it like a reproach or like some list of chores I would never get to. I could treat it as a list of "lovely opportunities." One quiet morning I sat down and asked myself the question, "What's really important to me?" I was flooded with thoughts and feelings and spent the next hour so deeply immersed in the process that I felt as if I'd disappeared from the earth.

What emerged was a real list of things that I truly believed were important to me—and the list sort of ordered itself so that I could see clearly what was *most* important to me—my health. I haven't felt healthy in the longest time, and I could see that everything else I want to do in life connected to me feeling healthier. So, I pulled that life purpose choice from the list and decided to focus just on it. And that's what I've been doing. Not only has my health been improving, but something in me has settled. I feel less anxious and chaotic. Maybe soon I'll get to some other of my life purposes, but for now, focusing this way is plenty!

Like Robin, life may be difficult at the moment for you, even overwhelming. Do the best you can. Maybe, like Robin, you can pluck one life purpose choice off your menu and focus on it. See if that's possible.

JOURNAL PROMPTS

1. Describe a "simple plan" for living your life purposes.

2. If you've created your list or menu of life purpose choices, which one would you like to choose as your number one priority? What's your top priority at the moment?

3. Describe your plan for paying attention to, and tackling, that top priority life purpose choice.

Live Your Life on Purpose | 237

JOURNAL PROMPTS

Chapter 39

DISMISS APOLOGISTS

Sometimes family members are in agreement that father or mother is a bully. Just as often, there is divided opinion. The oldest child may have seen it all and may have a very clear picture of how cruel her father was, either to certain family members or maybe to everyone in the family. But the youngest child in the family may have a very different experience, at once more limited and maybe simply better, as her authoritarian dad may have mellowed over the years.

Sometimes these disagreements among family members can be as traumatic and upsetting as the bullying itself. You may be clear on what went on, and completely accurate in your understanding of it, but maybe your siblings, who were just as abused and harmed as you were, are in denial about their experiences...or have followed in the authoritarian's footsteps. If something like this has happened, family members may be demanding that you have "no right" to complain, that you should be "nicer" to dad, that your memories are false or contrived, and that you are being disloyal to the family, painting the family in a negative light, and being downright ungrateful.

If this has happened and family members are attacking you, apologizing for the bully by claiming that it "just wasn't as bad as you're making it out to be" or that "He had a lot on his plate" or that "His childhood was worse than ours," you will have to treat those family members just as you have to treat the bully himself or herself; employing physical distance, psychological distance, limited contact, and the other tactics we've been discussing to shelter yourself from further mistreatment. Insofar as they are pressing their false vision on you, they are bullying you too, and you need to protect yourself; and if and when it makes sense to you to do so, speak out in a loud, clear voice that they are wrong, that you do not agree, and that you do not intend to acquiesce to their version of events.

Alfred explained, "I'm one of three brothers. The eldest is just like our father. He's a complete bully. I can deal with him because I know exactly who he is. My younger brother is convinced that nothing bad ever happened in our house. When I say to him, 'Do you remember when dad busted the door to the shed?' or 'Do you remember when dad took Bobby out and beat him?' he looks at me like I'm insane. That's so hard to deal with! Part of me needs him to remember and needs him to corroborate my understanding of what happened. And I know that's never going to happen. That makes me very sad."

Jeanne shared: "My father keeps saying that my mother's bad behavior is a result of her 'mental illness.' To me, her mental illness looks like privilege, narcissism, and a cruel streak a mile long. She presents herself as a cross between a victim and an invalid, but she has a ton of energy for anything she wants to do, like traveling to the world's top resorts or yelling at me, and the only victims in sight are the people around her. My father is completely in her pocket, and he's really the bigger problem for me because I desperately want to shake him and scream, 'Are you really such an idiot!' But that's not true. That's not what I want to scream. What I want to scream is, 'How can you not take my side? I'm your daughter!' "

Maria found herself surrounded by apologists, each playing a different angle. Her grandmother claimed that nothing bad ever happened to the grandkids. Her grandfather agreed that certain "unfortunate things" may have happened, but believed that there were reasons and that she should "forgive and forget." Her older sister blamed Maria, charging her with being "a really difficult child" who was "always stirring things up" and "never behaving properly." Her younger sister presented their parents as saints, as dirt-poor immigrants who had "overcome all the odds" and fashioned the American dream with themselves and their children. All of this made Maria physically sick, and hardly a sunrise dawned when she felt well enough to live her life fully or happily.

What can you expect? Realistically, that the person holding these false views will not change his mind, no matter what evidence you might be able to produce. Evidence will not matter. You can expect to be gaslighted and scapegoated, you can expect to be ganged up on, you can expect to be made to feel guilty and set up for humiliation, you can expect to be made to feel crazy, as if only an insane person could possibly hold your point of view. You can expect anger, estrangement, and all sorts of acting out, ranging from family members refusing to come to your child's birthday party to being written out of the will. Apologists are motivated by powerful reasons, both practical and psychological, for maintaining their version of the "big lie," and little they say or do should surprise you.

Your best responses are the same ones you would use to deal with the bully himself or herself. Protect yourself. Know that what you saw happen really happened. Enlist any allies you can, both from outside the family, and, if they exist, from inside the family. Limit contact to only those occasional visits and essential interactions. Be aware of what will trigger you and how you will deal with those triggers, either by sidestepping them or by having your plan in hand for recovering. Keep to your truth and do not waver. And create as good a life as you can, one that, by its richness and goodness, counteracts all this ganged-up bullying.

JOURNAL PROMPTS

1. Have certain family members sided with the bully?

2. What has your experience been like dealing with or being subjected to these collaborators?

3. How would you like to handle things differently?

Chapter 40

CALL BULLIES ON THEIR ATTITUDES AND BEHAVIORS

Some small but significant percentage of the victims of family bullying who have shared their stories with me have indicated that saying some variation of "No!" and "That's not okay!" to the parental bully caused them to moderate or even stop their behaviors.

Alice explained, "My mother always screamed at me. So, I would try to find some summer camp to attend just to get away from home. It didn't matter what the camp was offering—music, swimming, whatever—I would go. One summer when I was about twelve, I went to a camp that had these 'talking sessions'—I guess it was actually some sort of group therapy or encounter group or peer counseling, I don't know what. I found myself telling my story. A boy I kind of liked blurted out, 'Scream back!' When I got back home I did just that. My mother started screaming at the mess I'd made of my clothes and I got into her face and shouted, 'Stop screaming at me!' And she did! The screaming stopped. It was like she woke up from a trance."

Imagine that you want to say something to your bullying mother or father but your message is longer and more elaborate than just "Stop it!" Maybe it's that you're feeling bullied into a profession or feeling bullied into a marriage. Here's the process for calling out your parental bully in such situations:

1. Write out what you want to say. This may take multiple drafts since we don't usually say things well the first time that we try to articulate them. Stay calm, breathe, and get your thoughts down. It doesn't matter if it's all a jumble to begin with—that's to be expected. Stay with the process until you've gotten clear on what you want to say.

2. Meet objections. As you do this preliminary writing, think through what your father or mother is going to throw back at you. You know all their arguments already—it won't be hard to conjure them up as you think about what you want to say and how you want to meet their objections. Will there be the ones about "shaming the family" or "not trusting your elders"? Consider how you'll want to respond to those familiar objections.

3. Practice in the mirror. Once you've got your talking points articulated clearly on paper and in your own mind, practice saying them out loud. Practice in front of the mirror, walking around the lake, with your best friend, or any way you like, but do practice. Rehearsing does three jobs: It reduces our performance anxiety, strengthens our ability to articulate what we want to say, and strengthens our resolve.

4. Predict consequences. Picture what might happen if and when you present your case. You likely have a good idea of what the range of consequences might be. Although it may prove painful and daunting to picture the worst possible consequences, like a beating or a complete rupture and

estrangement of the relationship, it is good to be real about what might happen so that you make the best judgment possible as to whether you will or won't deliver your message. So far, you haven't committed to delivering it, just to preparing it: but the time is approaching when either you do speak or you don't.

5. Have a plan ready for dealing with those consequences. If you do intend to speak, and if you can predict or guess what the consequences may be, what will you do to deal with those possible consequences? Have an ally present so that physical violence is less likely? Make your case in a public place where it's less likely that your parent will make a scene? Be prepared to leave for a few days and stay at your best friend's house until the shock waves have subsided? Have a plan ready.

6. Pick a time and a place. Decide in your own mind when the best time will be to deliver your message, where the best place will be, who ought to be present, perhaps including an ally of yours, and who shouldn't be present, like your sister who always sides with your father. You may not be able to achieve perfection here, as it may not prove possible to orchestrate the perfect time, place, and situation. Just be mindful and do the best you can.

7. Expect to feel anxious. You are going to feel anxious as this confrontation approaches. Expect that, and, if you can, don't use that anxiety as an excuse to avoid the impending moment. If you hear yourself saying, "This is making me just *too* nervous!" try to talk yourself down from that flight reaction by reminding yourself that *of course* this was going

to prove taxing and anxiety-producing. Hopefully you have an anxiety-management technique at the ready to help: a breathing technique, cognitive technique, or somatic technique that has become a sturdy tool in your self-care toolkit.

8. Deliver your message. The time has come. Breathe. Show up. Speak your mind. Stand your ground. Say exactly what you intended to say. Don't back down, water your message down, nervously apologize, or in any way give in or give up. This isn't a negotiation. You aren't trying to "get somewhere." The goal is to call your bullying father or mother out on his or her behaviors and attitudes. Do that.

9. Forgive yourself if you can't quite deliver your message. If you weren't able to face the moment, make a new plan. Be easy on yourself. Nothing about this is easy. If you get to the front door of your parents' house and find yourself back in your car driving home, don't badmouth yourself. Congratulate yourself on getting as close as you did to a really hard confrontation. And, when you can, make a new plan. Maybe your new plan will include bringing an ally or writing out what you want to say, to have in your pocket. Create a new plan.

10. Deal with the consequences. If you manage to deliver your message and call out your bullying parent, maybe no negative consequences will ensue. Maybe a miracle will happen and your parent will see the light. But, more likely, you'll find yourself on the receiving end of exactly the consequences you predicted. You made a plan to deal with those consequences—who you'd call, who you'd visit,

which twelve-step meeting you'd attend—and now it's time to follow that plan. This wasn't easy—make sure to take care of yourself!

If you decide to call out your parental bully on his or her behaviors or attitudes, the above is a sensible plan to follow. It won't fully protect you or spare you grief—what could? Nothing can make genuinely hard things easy. But it can help!

JOURNAL PROMPTS

1. Is there something for which you really need to call out your bullying mother or father? What is that?

2. What's your best plan for doing that? The plan that I outlined above, or some other plan?

3. Write out what you want to say. See if you can hone your talking points.

Chapter 41

PRACTICE RESILIENCE

Resilience is holding a certain intention and then acting in alignment with that intention. The intention is to get off the mat in a habitual, practiced, and skillful way. One simple but effective way to become more resilient is by adopting the phrase "Sooner rather than later" as one of your mantras. What you are suggesting to yourself as you employ that phrase is that it is possible to get over something toxic—painful feelings, an episode of despair or high anxiety, a misstep or a mishap—more quickly than you might be accustomed to getting over such blows. This strategy, while simple, can nevertheless prove surprisingly effective.

Say that you encounter someone who triggers you—maybe it's your bullying stepfather. You feel terrible accidentally running into him at your son's Little League game. Your day is ruined, and when you get home, shaking and upset, you find yourself taking to your bed. However, by remembering to internally whisper, "Sooner rather than later," you may perhaps be able to spare yourself losing the whole week to upset. This is the essence of resilience: not becoming immune to inner pain, which is impossible, but recovering from hurt as soon as you can. The phrase "Sooner rather than later" might serve you beautifully.

Donna shared: "I've adopted the phrase 'sooner rather than later' in different parts of my life. I run my own business, and it's got a thousand moving parts. When something comes in that I can't attend to instantly, I will say to myself, 'Sooner rather than later,' which helps me get to it as soon as I possibly can. The same with emotions. I'm constantly fighting with my elderly mother about her driving—she needs to stop driving. Being the narcissist that she is, she sees herself as youthful and competent—as if. Every time we have one of these fights, I find myself super agitated. I get out of there as fast as I can, while telling myself that I owe it to myself to forget about Mom's nonsense 'sooner rather than later.' I can't help staying agitated for a while, but it does pass pretty quickly."

A second way to increase resilience is by staying oriented toward your life purposes. If you keep focused on what's important to you—fighting for a cause, loving your family, engaging in self-care, doing the next right thing—that will tend to force you to bounce back from blows and dark thoughts. If, for instance, you're feeling down, but you remind yourself that because you believe that you have something valuable to offer, you are adamant about building your business, that reminder is likely to cut through your mood and help you resume your heartfelt work.

Leonard explained:

> I grew up in a small settlement just off the high road between Santa Fe and Taos. It was a poor community, with lots of drinking, lots of spousal abuse, and lots of rage. I took the bus to school, and that was the best time of the day, riding the bus, not having to deal with my father, not having to deal with anything, just listening to my music.

When I got older, I joined the military to get away. That was a difficult experience, but I survived it. Finally, in my twenties, I began to see my life's path, and I became a teacher. That gave a sense of purpose every single day. If I had to encounter my father, who by that time was dying from his drinking but was taking a long time to die, I would picture my second-grade kids and remember my purpose. That would help me get over whatever got stirred up in me by having to deal with my father. I simply refused to let those feelings infect my teaching!

A third tactic is to mindfully reduce the stress in your life. The fewer things you have to bounce back from, the better. There may be stressors in your life that you can't rid yourself of right this second, stressors like an exhausting job, an unfulfilling marriage, or trauma consequences like anxiety and despair. But you can endeavor to free yourself of them over time. And while you are doing that brave work, you can choose some smaller stressors to try to eliminate right now.

Olivia explained:

Too many things have been going on, and when something stops working—something like the dishwasher breaking, or losing computer files, or getting into a fender-bender—that becomes the straw that breaks my back. That's been happening far too often, the physical and mental setbacks from things not working. The only thing I could think of to do was to try to simplify my life—to make simplicity my religion.

For instance, now I make simpler meals. And in fact, they're much healthier for me. Baking a piece of salmon and some vegetables may not sound like a life-changer, but keeping it that simple is making a difference. I grew up in a chaotic house, and I can't let my life get that chaotic. Simplify, simplify, simplify—that is the key to me staying on my feet and getting back on them if I stumble.

Resilience starts with an intention. The effects of trauma can leave us demoralized, anxious, and defeated; and unless we hold the intention to create our own morale, manage our anxiety, and rise up from defeat, we can become paralyzed and stranded. Is it your intention to keep bouncing back? If it has not been, cultivate that intention. It's on your shoulders to create and hold that intention because no one can do that work for you. Likewise, it's on your shoulders to do whatever it takes to realize your intention as only you can take action on your behalf.

Ignore an infant long enough, and as resilient as it may have been at birth, after a time, it will sink and succumb to what is called "failure to thrive." It may even die. Our native resilience can and does get depleted, and in order to heal from trauma and live well, we must skillfully rebuild it. What one new strategy might help you increase your resilience? If an answer comes to you, that is a strategy for you to learn, practice, and use. If you happen not to land on an answer, just stay open to both the question and the suggestion embedded in the question that there are strategies available to you that can help you.

JOURNAL PROMPTS

1. Are you less resilient than you would like to be? Do you connect that shortfall to the bullying you experienced?

2. What currently helps you bounce back from blows?

3. What new strategies might you like to try to increase your resilience?

Chapter 42

MANY WAYS UP THE MOUNTAIN: THINK FLEXIBLY

Asking the question "What should I do?" is a kind of ingrained cultural or even species-wide mistake because it makes us believe that there is one and only one right course of action with regard to any problem or challenge, like dealing with our bullying parent or healing from trauma.

The better question to ask ourselves instead of "What should I do?" is, "Of the many things that I might try, which one would I like to try first?" By imagining that there is only one correct thing to try—only one single thing that will help with our healing, help relieve our despair, or reduce our experience of anxiety—we limit ourselves to opting for the first answer that comes to mind.

Often that answer is the one we hear about the most, maybe the most culturally accepted answer, and so we never try any of the excellent alternative solutions that might be available to us. In order to heal from the effects of trauma, we want to be resourceful and do a good job of identifying and choosing from the many options available to us, rather than supposing that there is one "royal road" to healing.

Something traumatic has happened. There isn't one perfect thing to do to help a person heal from that terrible experience. A support group might help. A supportive therapist might help. A self-defense class might help. Writing about it in a journal might help. Writing about it as a memoir might help. Creating an online service that helps other survivors might help. Moving across town might help. Moving to another town might help. Sharing your experiences in a series of blog posts might help. Self-care and self-love, perhaps implemented by creating and using affirmations, might help. Is one of these guaranteed to help? No. Might any of these prove really valuable? Yes, it might.

Frank explained:

> I was seventeen and a junior in high school. My father was pressing me—bullying me—into getting a job and letting go of any idea of going to college. He saw college as useless, expensive, and even evil. I would meet the wrong sorts of people there, and I would start acting "high and mighty." He wanted to make sure that I understood my station in life and who my "real friends" were. It wasn't even that I really wanted to go to college all that much—but I wanted the option. I kept thinking, "What should I do about this?" and found myself getting nowhere.
>
> Then came a moment when I had to sign up for some high school senior year classes and could pick either those that would help me get into college—that would look good on my transcript—or take easier things. My dad wanted me to take easier things so that I would have more time to work after school. I was on the fence. Again, I kept thinking, "What should I do about this?" Finally, I went to a teacher I liked and

explained the situation. She sat me down and said, "If you didn't see this as black and white, choosing to take AP calculus or not take AP calculus, how would you think about this?" I took that question away with me and thought about it.

To begin with, nothing came to me. I kept coming back to either/or. I was stuck on take it or not take it. What other option could there be? Then it struck me that I could do both. If my dad's main agenda was that I work more, then I would work more—and take AP calculus. That put the burden on me to do both, and that also meant that I would need to stand up to my dad and say, "I will work more hours, but I'm also taking AP calculus because I don't want to rule out going to college." That felt scary—but strong. And that's exactly what I did. It took me many tries before I mustered the courage to tell my dad my plan, but finally I did—and he couldn't really find a way to poke holes in it.

He yelled, as usual, and gave me his "you'd better not forget who you are" tirade, but in the end, what could he say? That was the right option, adding work hours and taking the class, and really a completely obvious choice, and yet I could only see it when I let go of the idea that I had to choose between one or the other. The whole experience was liberating—and really, really useful.

There is some evolutionary influence on us that may cause us to suppose that there is only one answer per problem. Because we do not like to invite in the experience of anxiety, and because trying to choose among many options increases our anxiety, we unconsciously limit our choices in order to spare ourselves anxiety. But by operating that way, we also live far less resourcefully than if we expanded our horizons and identified multiple options. One or several of those other options might ultimately prove more beneficial than our first choice.

Here is the cognitive change to make: Instead of thinking "What should I do?" which implies that there is only one right course, substitute, "Which of the many things that I might try do I want to try first?" To keep this simpler, and thus more doable and more accessible, you might reduce "Which of the many things that I might try do I want to try first?" to "Which of many?" Trying substituting "Which of many?" for "What should I do?" That will help replace despair with hope and limitation with possibility.

JOURNAL PROMPTS

1. Describe in your own words the shift from "What should I do?" to "Which of many?"

2. Does that strike you as a useful tactic?

3. Remember a situation from the past. How might using this cognitive switch to reframe your thinking have benefited you back then?

Chapter 43

THE AUTHORITARIAN WOUND QUESTIONNAIRE

I've been interested in the authoritarian personality and particularly authoritarians in the family literally since I was a child growing up, when I saw the extent to which my little friends were being bullied by their parents. I grew up with a non-bullying mom and felt blessed not to be experiencing what my friends were experiencing. Later, in my teens, when I read the existential philosopher Jean-Paul Sartre's autobiography *The Words*, in which he thanks his lucky stars that he hadn't had a father, someone who likely would "lain full-length on me," as Sartre put it, I nodded in complete agreement. I didn't need one of those, either.

As a family therapist and a coach, I've worked with countless clients who've shared their experiences with me. I've read the literature on authoritarian personality and know those findings and themes. But the biggest learning for me has been the information I've received from individuals who've found my Authoritarian Wound Questionnaire in cyberspace, filled it out, and given me permission to share their stories with you. Those have been eye-opening!

You may be curious to see what this questionnaire looked like. Here it is. It is very straightforward. If you feel moved to respond to it, by all means feels free to do that. You may want to do that just for yourself; or you may also want to share your story with me, so that I can pass it on and help other victims and sufferers. If you do want to send it along to me, just fill it out and email it to me at ericmaisel@hotmail. com. Here is the Authoritarian Wound Questionnaire (without any of the simple instructions that accompanied it):

AUTHORITARIAN WOUND QUESTIONNAIRE

1. Have you had the experience of having to deal with an "authoritarian personality": a parent, sibling, mate, adult child, spiritual leader, coworker, boss, etc.?

2. What was that experience (or those experiences) like?

3. Authoritarian personalities are typically described as either "authoritarian leaders" or "authoritarian followers." What's your intuition as to whether the authoritarian in your life was more an "authoritarian leader" or more an "authoritarian follower"? Why do you think that?

4. Sometimes an authoritarian parent is described as "having an authoritarian parenting style." Which seems truer to you, if the authoritarian you're discussing is a parent: that he or she had an "authoritarian personality" or an "authoritarian parenting style"? That is, was the person in question more

an authoritarian "through and through" or did it seem like he or she was adopting a particular "parenting style"?

5. What would you say were the personal consequences of having been wounded by an authoritarian? (There are many common consequences, but I don't want to name them, as that will "put ideas in your head." I'd rather you think through what you believe those consequences to have been.)

6. What (if anything) has helped you deal with or heal from this "authoritarian wound"?

7. If you've been in therapy or counseling, has the issue of "dealing with an authoritarian personality" come up and been addressed? Has therapy or counseling helped in this regard?

8. If you've received a "mental disorder" diagnosis of any sort, do you see any relationship between having been wounded by an authoritarian and the symptoms that led to that "mental disorder" diagnosis?

9. If you had to make a complete break with the authoritarian in your life, what effect did that have on you, either positive (e.g., you felt safer and saner) or negative (e.g., feelings of loss and guilt)?

10. If you are still dealing with an authoritarian, what (if anything) helps you cope?

11. What advice would you like to share with those individuals who, like yourself, have been wounded in this way?

12. Please add anything you'd like to include about living with, working with, or dealing with an authoritarian and/or healing (or not healing) from the authoritarian wound.

_____

While we do not know where these millions upon millions of authoritarians come from, ready at what amounts to the drop of a hat to administer massive electroshock to their fellow human beings in "learning experiments," to feverishly follow a fascist, or to treat their children barbarically, they are right at this moment doing their damage behind closed doors. When circumstances allow, they are also doing that same damage brazenly in public. Because there are so many of them—researchers estimate that they may amount to as much as 25 percent of the population—the amount of harm they do is monumental. Whole societies have reaped the whirlwind, as have countless families.

According to my clients and respondents, it turned out that to just about a person, nothing had really fully worked to help them heal their authoritarian wounds or resolve the consequences of their traumatic experiences. Most aspired to healing, made efforts at healing, and were still hopeful about healing. But they knew that they were not "there" yet—typically not by a long shot. Many expressed the belief that they would never fully heal.

To my mind, this means the following for helpers, if you happen to be a therapist, coach, social worker, or other professional helper. First, many of your clients may be deeply pessimistic about the possibility that they will get any real help from you, given that they believe that they are broken, ruined, and doomed. Second, for those clients who retain some hope of healing and who see themselves on a journey of healing, they will deeply appreciate examining the issues I've been describing, even if that examination proves painful. They are primed to see this healing journey as a long one, they are likely to prove very patient and very accepting of small gains, and they know that this is work that they must do.

As an aside, as many respondents identified their mother (or some other female, like their grandmother) as being the authoritarian in their family as identified their father (or some other male). The same was true with respect to the world of work, where as many respondents reported authoritarian female bosses as reported authoritarian male bosses. I found this result surprising—but only at first glance. At second glance, it helps explain why women can be as staunchly fascistic as men when fascism gets a toehold in society. This is truly a species-wide problem.

There is a lot that I haven't covered in this slim book. For one thing, we haven't looked much at cross-cultural differences and the roles that society, culture, religion, and other social forces play. It may well be the case that a lot of authoritarian behavior is the result of cultural and societal norms. If your whole society prizes a certain value, like unquestioning obedience, then it follows that the majority of members of that society would be likely to be "strict" and "tough" on others and very easy with bullying. Parental bullying is an individual matter, and the bully in question is responsible for his or her actions. But there are societal forces at play, too—often dramatic ones.

As I mentioned earlier, I think it would be sensible to formally add parental bullying and authoritarian wounding to our current list of adverse childhood experiences. The adverse childhood experience literature has focused on ten adverse experiences that contribute to long-term psychological and emotional difficulties: physical abuse, sexual abuse, emotional abuse, physical neglect, emotional neglect, violence toward the mother, household substance abuse, household mental illness, parental separation or divorce, and the incarceration of a household member. Shouldn't parental bullying and authoritarian wounding join this list?

I hope our discussion has proven valuable. Feel free to be in touch with me at ericmaisel@hotmail.com. I wish you peace, healing, and freedom from bullying.

JOURNAL PROMPTS

1. Where would you like to go next in your thinking about parental bullying or your journey of healing from it?

2. What is your top takeaway from our discussion?

3. If you are dealing with a parental bully, try drawing up a plan for dealing with him or her. Good luck creating and implementing your plan!

Afterword

Have you recognized one or both of your parents in these pages? Have you recognized yourself?

Many of the stories presented here are truly harrowing. I could have included many, many more, including even more harrowing ones. The ones in these pages haven't been sanitized or censored. Real people have suffered in this way. If you, too, have suffered this way, I want to acknowledge and validate your experience. Yes, it all happened. Yes, it was terrible. Yes, you deserved none of it.

If you would like to share your experiences with me, I would be honored to receive your thoughts. You can be in touch with me at ericmaisel@hotmail.com or share your thoughts as part of a review you might decide to write and post on a book website or on your favorite social media outlet. If you do decide to write and post a review, I would love to hear about it; just drop a line to my email and let me know. Let's do the best job we can do revealing our truth and letting others know that they are not alone. You can also stay in touch with me by visiting my website, www.EricMaisel.com, or by connecting with me on social media:

via Instagram: @ericmaisel

LinkedIn: Eric Maisel

X: @ericmaisel

Facebook: www.facebook.com/eric.maisel

What now? Well, change, growth, and healing are possible. Please do have faith in the possibility that you can get your parent out of your head, that you can deal with family events more calmly (or skip them with less guilt), that you can bring self-awareness to your choices and your behaviors and not repeat destructive patterns, that change can happen, that growth can happen, and that healing can happen.

We can't simply snap our fingers and make all that materialize, although new understanding, new awareness, and new resolve can come in an instant. This is a human-sized miracle that sometimes happens, that we suddenly see where before we had a blind spot, that we suddenly feel up to saying something that previously we were too afraid to say. Luckily, that can happen in the blink of an eye.

But it's more likely that time will be required. That time is built into the tools and tactics I've shared in this book. It takes time to practice calm self-awareness and self-care, it takes time to release guilt and shame, it takes time to practice resilience and to create psychological separation. Take that time. May you continue on your healing journey, and may your path get less rocky each step of the way.

About the Author

Eric Maisel has written more than fifty books and has edited an additional dozen. He is the lead editor for the Ethics International Press Critical Psychology and Critical Psychiatry series, his Psychology Today blog *Rethinking Mental Health* has more three million views, and, in conjunction with Noble-Manhattan Coaching, he has developed a pair of worldwide training programs, a Creativity Coach Certificate Program and an Existential Wellness Coach Certificate Program.

Dr. Maisel regularly blogs for The Good Men Project and Fine Art America, presents sponsored workshops, webinars, and keynotes, and maintains an international coaching practice. He has been interviewed more than five hundred times on the topics of creativity, life purpose, meaning and mental health, and is currently developing a life organization app to be released in 2025.

Mango Publishing, established in 2014, publishes an eclectic list of books by diverse authors—both new and established voices—on topics ranging from business, personal growth, women's empowerment, LGBTQ studies, health, and spirituality to history, popular culture, time management, decluttering, lifestyle, mental wellness, aging, and sustainable living. We were named 2019 *and* 2020's #1 fastest growing independent publisher by *Publishers Weekly*. Our success is driven by our main goal, which is to publish high-quality books that will entertain readers as well as make a positive difference in their lives.

Our readers are our most important resource; we value your input, suggestions, and ideas. We'd love to hear from you—after all, we are publishing books for you!

Please stay in touch with us and follow us at:

Facebook: Mango Publishing

Twitter: @MangoPublishing

Instagram: @MangoPublishing

LinkedIn: Mango Publishing

Pinterest: Mango Publishing

Newsletter: mangopublishinggroup.com/newsletter

Join us on Mango's journey to reinvent publishing, one book at a time.

Printed in the USA
CPSIA information can be obtained
at www.ICGtesting.com
JSHW032003050424
60627JS00005B/6

9 781684 814909